D0369779

GREAT LAKES
GHOST STORIES

HAUNTED TALES PAST & PRESENT

BY WES OLESZEWSKI

AVERY COLOR STUDIOS, INC.
GWINN, MICHIGAN

©2004 Avery Color Studios, Inc.

ISBN 1-892384-26-4

Library of Congress Control Number: 2003116654

First Edition 2004

Published by
Avery Color Studios, Inc.
Gwinn, Michigan 49841

Cover artwork by Susan Robinson

This book is dedicated to Tim Juhl. Research historian, wreck diver, pilot and most importantly–a friend.

TABLE OF CONTENTS

ACKNOWLEDGMENTS

An acknowledgements section for a book about ghost stories is tough to do. This is primarily due to the fact that almost all of the stories are about dead people or mysteries, and consist of hear-say information passed along by folks who do not want their names associated with the stories. Thus I can begin by thanking all of the folks who have met their fate on the Great Lakes over the years and who have been kind enough to return from beyond to scare the daylights out of the living, who then turned around and told me their stories.

There are, of course, some living folks who helped out a lot with this book. One of the names that I can mention is Neil Schultheiss the owner and webmaster of the boatnerd.com website. Neil was kind enough to allow me to run a news item on his hugely popular web site where I asked all of the Great Lakes boatnuts out there to send me their ghost stories. Neil's site is so popular that lots of stories came my way. I'm sorry that I could not use all of them, but those that I was able to follow up on made the book far more interesting. Additional thanks goes to all of you whose stories I could not use. Although most of those rejected tales were simply re-hashes of famed stories told by other authors, or just plain dumb, it was still a nice try on your part. I urge you all to go out and steal fresh stories and try again, or to seek professional help in the form of a good psychiatrist.

I'd like to say "thank you" to the kind folks at the Milwaukee Public library for their help in sorting through records and direction in investigation. Similar help was granted by the Great Lakes Historical Society.

Lastly I'd like to thank my family, my wife Teresa and my newborn daughter Anjelysa Akie Oleszewski. They put up with my stacks of papers and odd-ball inspirations to a point beyond anything I could ever expect.

FOREWORD

This is a book of hear-say. Unlike all of my other books which are historical narratives based on research and the cross checking of documented facts, ghost stories normally have no documentation to prove their validity. Normally a ghost story is a personal experience that is relayed from one person to another. So, the telling of such tales requires the author to temporarily hang up the research historian's hat and simply take the story at its face value, then relay it to you, the reader. The disclaimer being that the stories that you will find in this book are only as truthful as the person who reported them to the author of this text. Whenever possible I have tried to enhance the stories with as many documented facts as I can find. When I found that the person telling a given story was "less than fully credible" I removed their story from my consideration as well as the book.

Although these stories of things that go bump in the night and events that seem too frequent to be pure coincidence may be nothing more than hear-say, they are still fun to tell. One thing that I can attest to, as the author, is that the people who told me the stories that you find within these pages honestly believe their stories. In many cases the folks who passed their stories of ghosts on to me asked specifically that their real names not be published and that some locations be altered so as to protect their identities. This I have done and I give fair warning here that some of the names have been changed to protect the innocent.

Over the past decade, since my first book hit the shelves, I have met thousands of people who work and live in the region of the Great Lakes. I have become close to divers and historians alike and have had the pleasure of meeting scores of ordinary folks and have also been handed hundreds of their personal ghost stories. Some are easily explained, yet others are true mysteries. Not all of these ghost stories consist of translucent apparitions who drift around in the spooky darkness. Often the hauntings consist of things that these ghosts do to let us know that they are here. Among those who study shipwrecks, or those who dive and discover shipwrecks the talk in public is always quite factual and analytical, to keep up our images of professionalism. But when we gather together in private among our peers, we talk about ghosts in the same manner that you would talk about your neighbor. The hauntings on the lakes are that common.

What are these things that we call ghosts? To that question I do not have an answer, and one will not be found within the pages of this book. I do have a theory, however. Consider that 1,000 years ago humans thought that lightening was a spirit–something supernatural that came from someplace unknown and did things that no one could imagine. If you were to approach a main-stream scientist of that time and fetch a theory of ice particle convection in storm clouds and rubbing off free electrons, thus developing an electric charge and hence lightening, you would be considered a crackpot, or even worse, a heretic! Today, we know that lightening is simply static electricity and that there is nothing supernatural about it at all. The difference between then and now is that humans are a lot smarter now and our gained knowledge allows us to understand those flashes in the stormy sky. Perhaps it is the same way with ghosts. Maybe we, as human beings, simply are not smart enough yet to study and fully understand them. Perhaps ghosts are just as natural as static electricity and we as human beings are simply not smart enough at this point in time to understand them.

So it is, that for the time that it takes to read this book, you are asked to take a moment and hang up your shipwreck historian's cap and just read these tales of ghosts and the people that have been haunted by them, and allow a moment for a cold shiver or a small smirk to haunt you. Although these stories may not be good for serious research, you will find them good indeed for telling around the campfire. No matter if you consider the tales in this text to be true or not, they are still fun to read and fun to retell in a darkened cottage by the lake on a stormy night.

THEY'RE BITIN'

Vic was never concerned much with Great Lakes shipwreck history. In fact, the things that had taken place out on Saginaw Bay nearly a century earlier were never in his thoughts. He would not have known a schooner from a lumber hooker if he had walked upon the deck himself. Vic's only interest in the lakes had always been the shining fish that could be caught within their waters and how often he would be able to take his little boat out and cast in his line. Indeed he was a sport fisherman and it was his passion. Whenever his mind went adrift, thoughts always went to images of rocking in his speedboat as it rested out on the lake and getting that big bite that would allow him to reel in another catch. Simply the rumor of "they're biting" was enough to send him heading toward a public boat launch and away from the world of everyday life.

It was the early 1960s and Vic was one of the countless factory workers employed in the Saginaw Valley. The manufacturing and auto industries in the United States were booming and there was plenty of work everywhere for anyone willing to get sweat on their brow and dirt on their hands. Vic's place of work was the Gray Iron Foundry and his shift of preference was the "third trick" or midnight to eight a.m. shift. This shift always left time for some early morning fishing after work or, if they were biting, it allowed him to try and skip out early and get some really good fishing in. Vic had a special arrangement going with his foreman so that when the fish were biting he could leave work early and the foreman would simply punch Vic's time card at the end of the shift so that the wayward worker would get paid for the whole day. It was an action that could get them both fired, but in an operation as big as the foundry, no one was ever going to notice. It was also an action that resulted in the foreman often receiving a hefty bundle of fresh perch filets when Vic's talents in the art of fishing paid off.

As the lunch horn sounded and Vic knocked off from his toil and headed toward the break table the din of factory noise continued to fill the air. From his locker Vic grabbed his sandwich bag and weather beaten thermos. As he eased onto the bench seat and propped his elbows atop the lunch table Vic took stock of his upcoming meal—a hot dog sandwich. You could always tell when it was the day before payday, because the cupboard and refrigerator were empty and lunch became anything that remained. In this case a couple of hot dogs had been sliced lengthwise to the point where they could be laid out on bread as if they were actual lunch meat. It was better than nothing, and with a resigned chomp he took a bite out of the hot dog sandwich. At that moment, Vic had no

6

idea that he was about to be sent on an encounter with a horrifying ghost ship, miles away on open Saginaw Bay. The gears of that ghostly time clock were already turning.

No sooner had Vic began to chew on his sandwich than Kenny came and plopped his lunch bucket down across from him. Kenny was not the most popular guy in the shop. He rarely bathed and had a tendency to smell a lot worse that the other guys. Vic tolerated him because Kenny's brother owned a bait shop up in Michigan's thumb and often gave Vic good deals on tackle.

"What're you doing still here?" Kenny groaned.

"Why?" Vic responded with a cheek half full of hot dog sandwich.

"They're bitin'. I figured you'd have the boat hitched up and you'd be headin' up north by now." Kenny responded as he dug into his lunch pail. "I was talkin' to my brother yesterday and he says the perch are bitin' like crazy off Bay Port."

Replacing his sandwich into its bag Vic took a moment to ponder the news. A good fisherman knows when it's time to get out on the water and no sooner had Kenny passed the word on to Vic, he was on his way to his foreman.

"They're bitin' up off Bay Port." Vic whispered as he angled up to the supervisor.

"Gotcha'." The foreman responded with a wink. "Freeze mine for me this time okay?"

"You got it." Vic answered as he headed for the gate.

Vic's home was just a few miles from the foundry and getting there required little more than a quick drive across the 6th street bridge. He could get his boat hitched and on the road faster than a fire company can roll a pumper out and respond to a call. He had already stocked it with everything from tackle and poles to a waiting cooler into which a cold six-pack could be thrown from the garage refrigerator. In just minutes Vic was backtracking across the bridge and on his way up Michigan's thumb headed toward Bay Port.

Located midway up the western shore of Michigan's thumb, Bay Port is just as much a tiny cottage community today as it was in Vic's day. Vic stopped to wait for Kenny's brother to open the bait shop, he then obtained a bucket of minnows and an update as to where the perch were biting. The word was that they were hitting just about a mile and a half out and they seemed to be biting the best right at sunrise. Armed with that information and his bucket of "shiners" Vic made haste to Bay Port and the public boat launch. With an efficiency that few others could manage, Vic single-handily launched his boat and parked his car and trailer. Soon he was speeding toward the spot where the fish were biting in the hope of having his line in the water before the sun came up.

Daylight began to hint as Vic placed his line into the water and almost immediately had a bite. He hardly noticed the rain that began to fall as he pulled in a series of catches. Soon the rain shower turned into a thick cold downpour, the likes of which every fisherman welcomes. It was the kind of weather that really gets the fish to bite, and soon Vic was pulling them in nearly as fast as he could set the hook. They were good-sized fish and his catch bucket was rapidly

filling. Pulling his six-pack of beer from the cooler Vic took his opener and pierced one of the cans and after taking a swig he began filling the cooler with additional perch. This was the best he'd seen them bite in years and he hardly had time to start eating his hot dog sandwich from work.

Almost as quickly as the frenzy of perch catching started, it suddenly stopped. Vic sat there in the rain eating his sandwich and sipping on his beer and wondered if that was the end of the run. It was then that he heard a screeching in the distance. It was the familiar sound of sea gulls in a feeding frenzy. Vic thought it was odd that sea gulls should be flocking so far out from shore and he looked around trying to see where the birds were located. The rain had cut the visibility down to just a few dozen yards in any direction and he could not see a thing. His attention returned to his fishing pole and line, but the screeching of the gulls grew steadily louder as if they were coming closer. Suddenly, as if a cold breath had huffed on his neck, Vic realized that there was a presence behind him. Spinning around he was startled to see a big battered wooden boat just a few feet away. Instantly he thought that it was a commercial fishing boat and it was going to run him down, but the boat had its side to him. Overhead a huge flock of sea gulls swarmed and screeched their cry. The boat was very beaten up and old and Vic wondered who would be cheapskate enough to take such a tub out and use it for commercial fishing.

About then Vic noticed that, so far as he could see, there was no one on deck. There were only the sea gulls in a huge white swarm. Whatever they were feeding on was driving them crazy. Vic stood up and tiptoed on his boat's seat to try and see if there was anyone aboard this old wooden boat. It was then that he saw what the gulls were feeding upon. Lashed to the remains of the boat's broken mast was the body of a crewman. The gulls had pecked away his eyes and were now feasting at the sockets while their fellow birds were biting at the flesh of the corpse.

There is a kind of nightmare shock that overtakes the soul when a person meets a gruesome and horrible surprise. As if he's found a big spider crawling unexpectedly on his shoulder Vic jumped in near convulsion. His can of beer leaping from his hand, Vic's instinct was to get out of there before the gulls turned on him and pecked away his eyeballs too. Twisting madly at the key he managed to fire the outboard engine of his boat. He jammed the throttle forward and leaned ahead as if his posture may speed his craft. He did not look back.

Slamming against the dock, Vic's speedboat came to rest as he leaped from it. Slipping on the planks of the rain-soaked dock he came down hard on one knee and put a tear in his pants. That did not slow him down a bit as he dashed to his car and leaped into the front seat. His mind was spinning. "Those poor fellows," he thought of the men on the old boat. His hands were shaking and he felt sick. Reaching under the front seat he got the bottle of whisky that he kept under there for emergencies. If there was ever a time to take a belt, this was it. In fact, he took several belts from the jug before he began to settle down.

He had to notify someone about this horrible thing that he had just discovered. Surely someone out there must be missing that boat and the poor guy who was aboard. The image kept running through his mind of those gulls pecking into those eye sockets and biting at the flesh. What a horrible thing—Vic took a few more swigs of the whisky. Only then did he have enough wits about him to go back to the boat and get his car keys, which were attached to his boat key. Starting his car, Vic had no idea where to go or who to report this whole thing to, he just headed out and started driving along the highway.

With his mind still spinning and the whisky taking effect, Vic headed off into the rainy morning. Time seemed lost, but suddenly, coming in the opposite direction appeared the unmistakable blue car of a Michigan State Trooper. Vic nearly locked the breaks of his station wagon as he figured to turn around and get the trooper's attention. There was no need for Vic to try and gain the officer's attention, however, the trooper had watched as Vic's car stopped and turned and he was waiting. Vic met the trooper in a near state of panic and began babbling his broken story about the boat and seagulls.

"You been drinkin' buddy?" The officer frowned as Vic tried to make his point. "How many have you had?"

Vic's pleading became more intense as he settled into something that the trooper now saw as more likely to be fear and less likely be a drunken babble. After a protracted conversation the trooper offered to give Vic a ride back to the boat launch in an effort to further investigate his story. There were the caught perch, the empty beer can and the soggy hot dog sandwich and although the visibility out on the lake had improved, there was no sign of any big wooden boat with a dead crewman. With his investigative instinct satisfied that he was simply dealing with a fisherman who had one too many swigs of whisky, the trooper offered to drop Vic off at a local diner. Some coffee was probably the best cure for this situation in the officer's opinion. He warned Vic not to return to his car and try to drive until he had sobered up. The trooper assured him that he would pass Vic's concern on to the Bay City Coast Guard station and they would handle it from there.

THEY'RE BITIN'

After several cups of strong coffee Vic hitchhiked back to his station wagon and then recovered his boat. For the next several days he read the newspapers carefully, but never saw any mention of the old wrecked boat and the dead crewman. In the weeks that followed he told his story of the big old boat and the biting gulls several times at work, but soon it became sort of a joke among the guys and he took some ribbing. After that he did his best to only tell his story to those who may actually consider it to be as true as he believed it to be. He still loved to fish, but he avoided that spot off of Bay Port no matter how good the fish were biting.

What Vic never knew was that a boat such as the one he had come across on that awful morning actually existed and her name was *Joseph A. Hollon*. The reason why he never read anything in the newspapers about her was that he was looking in the newspaper almost a century too late. In the end of October 1870, the *Hollon* went missing in a storm on Lake Huron. Three days after she had been reported lost she was found drifting with three of her crew missing and the fourth "lashed to a pump, with his eyes pecked out by the sea gulls." The location where she reappeared was 25 miles west southwest of Pointe aux Barques, just off of Bay Port.

AMBER LAMPS

It was the summer of 1984 and Wil was, like most other confessed "boat-nuts," attempting to spend as many of those pleasant summer days near places where the lakeboats could be seen, heard and photographed. The result was that he had made a trip to Sault Saint Marie, Michigan and staked out a campsite at the county campground just above Mission Point. This camping area is commonly known among boat watchers as being one of the best places to stay and watch the big lakers slide past. Additionally, it is within easy walking distance of Mission Point itself. The point is a rock-studded bend in the Saint Marys River and also is the bottle neck of the Great Lakes. It is the single point where the greatest volume of lakeboat traffic passes in the closest proximity to dry land. Upbound and downbound traffic moving through the Soo locks must all squeeze past Mission Point and thus pose to have their picture taken by camera armed boatnuts. Both Mission Point and its nearby campground are the place to be if you are a fan of the giant oreboats that sail the lakes.

GREAT LAKES GHOST STORIES

Lake Superior stretches to the north and west of Sault Saint Marie and along its shores are the towns of iron ore. Places such as Superior and Ashland Wisconsin, Duluth and Two Harbors, Minnesota and Marquette, Michigan. These cities were founded on the mining of the rich iron ore that resides at the feet of their populations. Some, such as Ashland, no longer ship ore while others, such as Duluth ship vast quantities of the red gold. Others, like Superior, ship smaller quantities of ore than they have in the past. Then there are the Canadian ports for the grain harvested from the vast plains to the west. Traditionally, the lakeboats have hauled these cargoes as well as other assorted bulk products down across Lake Superior from the time that the ice began to break up in the spring until it reformed in the winter. Since 1855 lake vessels have been able to freely travel between Lake Superior and the lower lakes by way of the locks at Sault Saint Marie. These locks were constructed to by-pass the rapids of the Saint Marys River which runs along the Canadian and U.S. border and separates the cities of Sault Saint Marie, Michigan and Sault Saint Marie, Ontario. Starting with a pair of step locks in 1855, the system of locks at Sault Saint Marie, also known as "The Soo" has been constantly evolving and growing. In fact, with the beginning of the 21st Century, plans and work are underway to develop another new lock at the Soo. In a steady parade, countless vessels have passed upbound and downbound through the Saint Marys River and the Soo Locks. On many occasions, vessels have passed up toward Lake Superior, and never returned. Plenty a mariner has seen the lights of Sault Saint Marie disappear behind them and then the mariners themselves have disappeared. Still, this bottleneck of lakes commerce has always been a dandy place to go and watch the boats. Many a boat watcher has stood on the shore and watched the lakeboats pass while wondering about those that went missing up on Superior.

In keeping with his calling as a true boatnut, Wil awakened well before daylight and headed off to the campground shower. The objective being to get his daily hygiene duties out of the way in time to be able to use every second of daylight for taking photographs. By the time he exited the campground showers the sky was just beginning to brighten with the first hints of dawn. The only problem being that one of those famous Sault Saint Marie fogs was rapidly forming over the river. A bank of cotton mist was already hanging over the water. It extended from the surface to a height of about 60-feet. At first Wil thought that his plan to get an early start was now wasted because the fog was sure to obscure any picture taking for the next several hours. Then, as he stood there contemplating the rapidly thickening fog, Wil noticed two dim masthead lights sticking up above the mist. The lamps were moving together and obviously attached to a single vessel that was totally obscured by the fog. He watched as the dim amber lamps moved slowly down the river toward Mission Point.

There was something odd about those lamps. Their hue was a strange amber color and the masts that they were mounted upon were spaced too closely together to be one of the big modern freighters, yet too far apart to be a tug or work boat. In his brain he scaled the lights and the distance between the masts and figured it to be between 350 to 450-feet. Wil knew by heart the size and shape of every lakeboat sailing and could normally identify a laker on the distant horizon simply by its silhouette. He could also sit by the campfire on the shore of the Saint Marys River and identify a given lake freighter by its lights. These lights, however, had him puzzled. There was no boat running in that size range–at least no boat that he was aware of. The longer he watched them slide by, the more he found himself wondering "Who is that?" Maybe someone has brought out some vessel that has been in lay-up for a protracted time. The year 1985 was the beginning of the recovery of lakes shipping following the 1980 recession and the near death of the steel industry. Most boat watchers had high hopes for the reappearance of some of the old time vessels and Wil was no exception. By the time that the lamps above the fog approached Mission Point itself, the fog bank swallowed them and Wil was left standing there, shower kit in hand and damp towel slung over his shoulder, alone in the pre-dawn darkness.

The mind of a true boatnut works fast when capturing a vessel is involved. Wil knew that "Soo Control", the center that directs vessel traffic on the Saint Marys River, would be talking by radio to every vessel on the river and the boat that had the strange lamps would be no exception. All along the river there are required reporting points, one of which was Mission Point and the next one downbound being Six

AMBER LAMPS

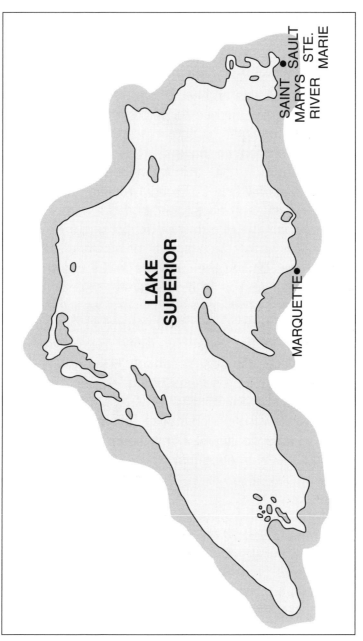

Mile Point. It was likely that the strange boat had already passed the reporting location at Mission Point, but she would have to call in again at Six Mile Point in about 33 minutes. Then he would know for sure who this odd boat was and could log her in his notebook. With a determined stride he made his way back to the camper. Plugging an earphone into his marine scanner so as to not awaken the rest of his camping kin, Wil turned the radio on and listened intently for Soo Control to speak. Soo Control did not keep him waiting very long. In fact, no sooner had Wil activated the scanner than its set of red LEDs stopped their march across the radio's face and lit on Channel 12. Soo Control was closing the river due to the fog and was informing all vessels in the system to stop and go to anchor until further notice. It sounded as if they were repeating a directive that they had made clear earlier and although the vessel captains may have been disappointed, Wil was delighted. His mystery boat could not have gotten more than a few hundred yards below Mission Point, and Soo Control would not normally allow fog-bound traffic to move again until the mist had lifted significantly. This meant that his mystery laker was now trapped just below Mission Point, and when the fog began to lift, she would be easy prey for his camera.

As the morning passed, the fog grew thicker. Will ventured out toward Mission Point on foot to see if he could see through the fog and solve the puzzle of the amber lamps. Standing on the riverbank, he could only see a few feet out onto the river. Picking up a rock he tossed it gently and heard it plunk into the water, but never saw a ripple. Hiking farther down the river, Wil hoped to perhaps hear something of the vessel. Perhaps crew talking on deck or machinery being rattled about. Sometimes vessels can be identified by their sound. Such was always the case of the *Silver Isle.* With her engine making a continued and rhythmic, dull "thump" a good boatnut could tell she was coming long before she came around the bend in any confined waterway. Yet, as Wil stood on the mist shrouded riverbank, his ears were cheated as not a sound came from the distance. He knew that this sort of fog could likely hold on well into the afternoon and so he headed back to the campsite to listen to the scanner and study his well worn copy of "Know Your Ships 1985."

In the first hours of the afternoon, the fog suddenly began to show signs of dissipating. Such is the way with Saint Marys River fog, it lifts as fast as it sets. Wil did not wait around for Soo Control to begin releasing vessels. At the first hint of the fog beginning to lift he quickly gathered up all of the tools that every good boatnut is required to carry. In a single scoop he nabbed his camera, assorted lenses, binoculars and his "Know Your Ships" just in case his mystery vessel may be a "saltie" or a salt water vessel visiting the lakes. In a huff he marched to Mission Point and planted himself upon a large, damp boulder. There he waited as the curtain of mist rapidly began to melt away.

Dutifully he checked his camera's light meter and made sure it was ready to shoot. The identity of this vessel and its strange amber masthead lamps had puzzled him all day and now he was not only going to discover who she was, but he was also going to get some terrific photos of her to add to his collection, or so he thought. As the fog lifted and the river became more and more visible, Wil squinted into the remaining murk, but there was no boat there. In fact, when the fog had completely dissipated, and Wil could see all the way down to Six Mile Point, there were no downbound vessels to be seen at all!

Stunned the dedicated boat watcher began to run the possibilities through his mind. Perhaps the boat had run all the way down and around Six Mile Point and not told Soo Control. With that in mind he made his way back to the campsite and sat for the remainder of the day, glued to his marine scanner. That day, however, as Soo Control released vessels to move, there were no downbounders above Mud Lake, which is several hours sailing time below Mission Point. Only two boats passed and they were both 1000-footers whose deckhouses would have loomed above the fog. In fact, that entire day, there were no vessels of any sort reported operating in the Saint Marys River that were under the size of 647-feet long.

That evening as the campfires were lit and darkness settled in once more over Sault Saint Marie, Wil took plenty of ribbing about chasing a boat that wasn't there. That type of joking he did not mind, what haunted him was the memory of those two amber lamps sticking up just above the fog. They had the glow of old oil lamps and he recalled that looking upon them was like looking back through time. Perhaps he was right, perhaps he had been given a glimpse into the past. Perhaps one of those old boats who found a grave up in Lake Superior decided to finally make her passage down the river and then once again into eternity. And just perhaps he was the luckiest boatnut on the lakes that morning as he caught her passage. The more he thought about it, however, the more he began to regret one fact. On that one occasion, he had been caught without his trusty camera. Wil still visits Sault Saint Marie and camps out in the same campground each and every summer. He still monitors Soo Control on his marine scanner and he still gets his daily shower out of the way well before daylight, only now, he takes his camera with him to the showers.

A VOICE
IN THE FOG

This story was originally published in my previous book *True Tales of Ghosts and Gales* and although it is my personal policy not to repeat stories, this is an exception to that rule. The reason is that after that book had gone to print I found the single piece of information that I had been searching for during the entire production of that previous text. After nearly five years of research I discovered the name of the ghost and such information is so rare and so important that it requires me to repeat the story and inform my readers of the identity of this poor soul who is still out there, reliving a single moment of horror cast upon it by Lake Michigan. Thus, here, again, is the tale of the voice in the fog.

By the afternoon of Sunday, August 6th, 2000 the fog that had set in at Grand Haven, Michigan and was showing no signs of lifting. Out on Lake Michigan the conditions were just as thick, with visibility ranging from one quarter of a mile to one half mile. Overall it was a murky end to a fairly festive week in the harbor. The previous six days had been used to celebrate the

GREAT LAKES GHOST STORIES

76th Anniversary of the establishment of an annual Coast Guard Festival in that port city and the entire week had been dedicated to the keepers of valor–the United States Coast Guard. In attendance at the festival was the 180-foot buoy tender *Acacia*, the 140-foot ice-breaking tugs *Neah Bay* and *Mobile Bay* and most prominently, the flagship of the Great Lakes Coast Guard, the mighty 290-foot ice breaker *Mackinaw*. During daylight hours, the Coast Guard fleet was open to tours as proud crew members stood by. Still, all good times must come to an end, and so it was with the annual Coast Guard Festival. On that foggy Sunday the *Mackinaw* cast off her lines and headed out to attend to her duties.

Moving into the cotton fog the *Mackinaw* had her radar scanning the distance and extra crew were stationed on her deck to keep a sharp lookout. In fact, every crewman on duty was keeping a weather eye toward the lake. It would really look bad if while departing the Coast Guard Festival the pride of the lakes were to accidentally run down some unsuspecting pleasure craft. With that in mind, the pilothouse crew inched the big ice breaker silently across the glassy surface of Lake Michigan using all of the caution of a jeweler working on a fine watch. Well out onto Lake Michigan the big steel hull of the ice breaker slid along the surface without making more than a ripple as her commander directed her to be steered to the northwest. Like every other member of the crew on board the *Mackinaw* at that moment, the pilothouse watch had no idea that resting just over 100-feet beneath them were the bones of a long forgotten wooden lakeboat. Also resting beneath them were the memories and the spirits of a tragic night long ago when disaster was played out upon these same waters. It was a memory that would soon reach out and touch all of those aboard the *Mackinaw* in a haunting manner.

Just eight and one half miles northwest of Grand Haven, a crewman standing lookout heard a sudden cry coming from the lake. For a moment he thought he was mistaken, but then the voice cried out again. It was the voice of a child, the voice of a little boy out there in the distant fog, crying for help. Instantly the crew of the *Mackinaw* were called to alert and all off-duty crew were mustered on deck. The voice was heard again and it was certainly a little boy calling for help.

As with their predecessors in the United States Life-Saving Service, it is the sworn duty of every

Coast Guard ice breaker Mackinaw. *D.J. Story photo*

GREAT LAKES GHOST STORIES

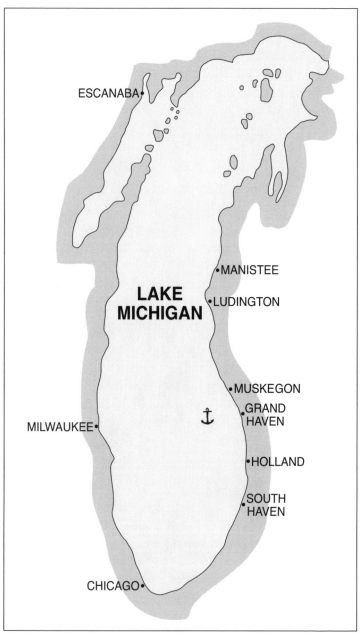

member of the Coast Guard to place their own lives in peril to save the lives of others and now their call to duty had come again. The *Mackinaw* began a standard search pattern as her crew strained their eyes and ears against the fog. Lake Michigan, however, frustrated their efforts and nothing was found. Now, Coast Guard station Grand Haven was notified by radio. Once again, like their life-saving forerunners, the station's crew manned their boat and charged to the rescue knowing only that somewhere out there a little boy was in the water calling for help. It is important to note that this was the era before the September 11, 2001 attacks on America and the annual assets budgeted to the Coast Guard were so thin that they were nearly invisible. Deploying a rescue boat meant spending some of those thin assets, and this was not an action done on a lark or on a hunch, the Coast Guard was convinced that there was a life in danger. So it was that the swift rescue boat was deployed and joined the *Mackinaw*. As the second boat arrived on the scene, the little boy's voice was clearly heard again, in the foggy distance calling for help. Now both Coast Guard vessels began to search. Approximately 1,000 yards from the center of the search area, a pleasure craft was found. The occupants of the pleasure boat had no children aboard and had heard nothing of the voice calling for help. Likewise, every other pleasure craft in the vicinity had heard nothing.

In the days that followed, no one reported anyone missing. There were no overdue pleasure craft anywhere on Lake Michigan and a check of local law enforcement showed no one reporting any loss of a child. All of the Coast Guard vessels returned to their stations and their crews resumed their duties. Officially, the Coast Guard simply states that "The case remains open." Officially, the Coast Guard can offer no explanation for the events of August 6th, 2000 and that is because they were actually searching in the right place, but in the wrong time. Indeed their deployment of assets was too late… 126 years too late.

Along the Milwaukee waterfront, the smell of horse manure hung heavy as Harry Lee's boots seemed to avoid the piles of droppings that were common on every street. It was a warm Saturday evening in the late summer of 1873 and Harry was on his way to a favored tavern after a hard day's toil at the Wolf and Davidson shipyard. With a swagger that was befitting his position as a foreman at the shipyard, Harry entered the darkened tavern and bellied up to the bar. Some of the boys on his crew were already there and a few sips ahead of their foreman. Flowing faster than the drinks, was the grumbling that the shipyard workers were spewing. As Harry's calloused hand gripped his glass he listened intently to the men as they vented. It was a situation that most shipyards would not force upon their workers and could actually be considered a sin. Both Harry Lee and his crew were being forced to, once again, work on Sunday and it was being caused by one boat, the *Ironsides*.

"I'm getting' mighty tired of workin' Sundays on that rotten *Ironsides*." Harry spouted aloud to a chorus of agreeing groans from his crew. "In the blasted dry dock, replacin' one plank at a time, when her whole stern is rotten."

A VOICE IN THE FOG

Harry sneered as he took a long drink and then wiped the excess from his whiskers. His crew grew silent as they waited for their foreman to continue to reflect their disdain.

Around the bar the talk soon resumed with most grumbling about William H. Wolf and Thomas Davidson themselves for being so greedy as to keep taking the *Ironsides* for these patch-up jobs. After all, the yard was well on its way toward its best year ever with the building of a tug, a steamer and six schooners, the bosses still insisted on taking these patch-up jobs. Everyone involved would lose their Sundays just so Wolf and Davidson could get that $1,000 for use of the dry dock. Foreman Lee, however, had other thoughts as he gazed toward the bottom of his glass. He knew that the real blame should be focused on Engelmann Transportation and the penny-pinching Mr. Engelmann himself.

"I'll tell ya' somethin' else," Harry blurted out, again silencing his crew's grumbling, "she'll go down soon because of those leaks in her stern." The crew growled in their agreement–then old Engelmann will get his due and the yard will be rid of both the *Ironsides* and her Sunday repair jobs.

Such scorn was not always associated with the *Ironsides*. In fact, prior to her employ in the hands of the Engelmann Transportation Company, the vessel was considered as being one of the finest on the lakes and that was a reputation that she still carried with the those who were not involved in her maintenance. When the boat entered service in 1864 she was one of the "Palace Steamers" whose job it was to carry immigrants west at minimal expense, yet carry the wealthy across the same waters in the greatest of luxury. Constructed at the Quayle and Martin yard in Cleveland, she measured 231-feet in length, 38-feet in beam and 14-feet in depth of hold. All of that girth gave her a registered tonnage listed as 937. Erected upon her deck at each of her beam ends were two huge arches, each reinforced with heavy iron plates and bolts. Between the arches, cross-beams extended to fasten the hogging structure as a single unit. Her first class cabins were designed to put any four star, shoreside hotel to shame. Splendid furniture with velvet covered cushions stocked every room, the floors of which were covered in plush Brussels carpeting. A total of 44 staterooms graced her lines and a large number of those rooms could be turned into family rooms. In the extreme forward end of the boat was a series of community washrooms. These were all graced with marble fixtures and a feature that for this era simply sang out with elegance–hot and cold running water. Another opulent feature was a room for taking baths. It too was equipped with hot and cold running water. On her deck, was located her main cabin with its grand room that ran nearly the length of the vessel. This room was an open hall that was used for both dining and socializing. At the aft end of the grand hall was a huge painting of the frigate *Ironsides* rendering aid to a burning British vessel. At the forward end of the grand hall was another huge painting. This second painting was of the Sault Rapids and the surrounding landscape.

Propulsion equipment of the *Ironsides* was supplied power from two huge boilers, each of which measured

21-feet long and 10-feet in diameter with 378 water return tubes. She was driven through the water by twin propellers each being nine feet in diameter. All of this appeared to be directed toward the task of moving passengers from the lower lakes to the wilderness ports of the upper lakes with ease and comfort. There was, however a secondary nature to the *Ironsides* at the time of her launching. She was also designed to be an oreboat. Into her sides, companionways had been constructed to allow the rolling on and off of barreled cargoes of iron ore. In 1864, the shipping of iron ore from the upper lakes was still somewhat of a novelty and the quantities that were needed were in little more than so many barrels at a time. Still, between ore and the goods that were needed to build the settlements of Lake Superior, freight was as important a cargo to the *Ironsides* as were passengers. Of course, the boat's crew would do all that they could to insure that the passengers felt that they were aboard a luxury steamer rather than a freighter and from the porters and cooks to the ship's musicians, everyone went out of their way to please the passengers who came aboard the new *Ironsides.*

Indeed she was a floating palace of the freshwater seas when she was launched. By the time that the boat got into the charge of Engelmann Transportation, much of the plushness of her accommodations were becoming worn. Still, her cabins were roomy and she wore her age well as far as the paying public could see.

When she was constructed, the question of safety was addressed by her initial owners, who required some state of the art safety features in her design.

Stanton drawing of the Ironsides. *Author's Collection*

From hoses for fire fighting to additional lifeboats, she seemed ready to handle any emergency The vessel's hull was divided into three sections by two "water-tight" bulkheads. Such multiple bulkheads were a rather unusual feature for her day and in 1864 no type of bulkhead was actually "water tight."

Between 1864 and 1873 there were great changes in the Great Lakes maritime industry. In the first years of the 1870s an economic recession had taken place that was bad enough to send some immigrants packing back to the old country. The flood of "pioneers" booking passage to the wilderness of Lake Superior had dwindled to the point where the *Ironsides* was no longer competitive in that trade. She changed hands several times and finally came into the service of the Engelmann Transportation line. The Engelmann brothers were in an up-start position against the Goodrich Transportation line. For several years they had been in the business of operating a small lumber fleet. They acquired a few well worn passenger vessels and transformed themselves into a passenger and freight line. Both the Engelmann Transportation line and the Goodrich Transportation line ran vessels out of Milwaukee to destinations on southern and eastern Lake Michigan. It was short-haul service that carried both passengers and cargo and the competition was cutthroat. Goodrich had the advantage in cash and docks, but Engelmann was determined to keep the edge by using less expensive vessels and saturation schedules. By 1873 the two companies were crisscrossing Lake Michigan, each going to different cities, but each competing for every warm body and cold piece of cargo that could be found in Milwaukee. Along the docks there were those who called Engelmann a skinflint with leaky boats who refused to invest a dime in his fleet. Of course there were those who would say the same about Goodrich. The fact is that this was the era of the robber-barons and it was also the era when there was very little regulation of vessels. The term skinflint could also be the difference between a successful business man and a failure. Using old boats and not investing your profits back into the fleet could spell disaster or be considered as shrewd. When disaster did strike, there was no government agency to step in and investigate. The Coast Guard would not be established for another four decades. So, normally, a blue ribbon panel would sit down and look into the matter. The members of such panels were robber-barons in the same circles as the vessel owner that they were investigating. Of course the game was rigged and the results of the investigation would likely point toward a drown captain rather than his robber-baron boss. Such were the times that found the *Ironsides* coming into Milwaukee harbor on Saturday, September 13, 1873.

Captain Harry Sweetman was nearly beside himself as the vessel hovered up to the dock at Milwaukee's West Water Street. Purser Sam Watkins had orders to see to it that the passengers disembarked through the forward gangway and not one stick of cargo was to be unloaded until the dock was cleared of passengers. He was also under orders that no stragglers were to be tolerated and every passenger was to be disembarked as swiftly as possible. Captain Sweetman's concern was justified. The *Ironsides* had wet her cargo, again, and he wanted to make sure that the word of this did not get out. A rumor that the boat was in a leaking condition could easily cause passengers to avoid her as well as the rest of the Engelmann boats and could spread like a poison around the port cities of Lake Michigan. The fact, however, was that the leaking was so bad that it had gotten ahead of the pumps this time and now the water in the aft cargo hold was nearly knee deep. By unloading the passengers through the forward gangway, they would not see the flooded compartment or the crew that was working feverishly to pump out the water. By not unloading the damaged cargo, there would be no way for the public to witness that mess either. It was a routine that the crew of the *Ironsides* had been through before.

A VOICE IN THE FOG

A phantom leak that no one could seem to find had plagued the *Ironsides* all season. The boat would leak severely when she was under way, but as soon as she was placed into dry dock, there would be no obvious area found that could cause such an intrusion of water. A few suspected areas would be caulked and a timber or two replaced, but as soon as she was back under power on the open lake, she would begin to take water. Although her owners would not face it, and her crew did not want to think about it, the fact was that this leak was not in one spot, but along her entire bottom. It is likely that her timbers were springing in almost every butt along her bottom and thus providing for millions of tiny inlets for water. Once the boat was under way, the normal stresses and torques from that activity would have opened up these tiny spots even more and caused a cumulative effect that bordered on her being a sinking vessel. In the dry dock, there would be no apparent sign of a gap that was big enough to cause a major leak. So the best that the repair foremen could do was to patch a suspected location and again tell the company that the boat's entire bottom needed to be repaired. The Engelmann's simply were not willing to invest the down time of the vessel, or the money required to have her entire bottom redone during the busy shipping season. They seemed content to ignore the problem and let the boat keep running. On the leg prior to the trip that the boat had just completed, she had leaked so badly that her cargo of wheat was damaged to the point where it could not be removed into the elevator by use of the Dart legs. Instead the wheat had to be shoveled out by hand and left on the wharf in Grand Haven to dry. Now on her return trip to Milwaukee the package freight had been damaged by the flooding. After the paying passengers had left the dock. The crew set to the task of removing the soaked cargo and placing it on the dock where it would hopefully dry out.

Beyond Captain Sweetman's headaches with the leaking condition of the *Ironsides*, were Chief Engineer Robert McGlue's woes. The leaking was always aft and had a tendency to work its way amidships into his engine room. McGlue and his crew were often working in knee-deep water and having a rough time keeping the boat's fires lit. Still, one who complained to often and too intensely to the front office would likely find himself without a job. In this era of unregulated robber-barons and robber-baron wanna-bes, such as the Engelmanns, a chief that had been dismissed for such complaints could find himself labeled as "troublesome" and thus unable to find another job on another boat. So, the good chief simply had to be content to grumble to himself in his cabin and telling his crew to just "pump her out" again. Using a combination of her steam pumps and some hand pumps, the crew worked well into Sunday afternoon to get the water out of the *Ironsides*. Then, in the eyes of the Engelmanns, she was ready for more paying passengers, more cargo and another trip across Lake Michigan.

At their small but comfortable home located at 310 Jackson Street, the family of Henry Valentine were just returning from church as the *Ironsides* was preparing to sail again. Henry kept close supervision as his wife Nattie changed the cloths of their four year old son,

A VOICE IN THE FOG

Harry, from his Sunday best to a cute little blue sailor suit. The garb was indeed proper, considering that the little boy and his mother were about to go sailing across Lake Michigan on the *Ironsides*. There would be plenty of time for dinner and then to pack some last minute items before heading out to the Engelmann dock. From their house it was a three block walk to Huron Street and then another three blocks up to the drawbridge and across it to the dock where they would meet the *Ironsides*. For several days the trip on the boat had been the subject of excited conversation between the four year old and his parents and as they left home for the boat, he led the way well ahead in his excitement. As the Valentine family came to the bridge they could see the *Ironsides* docked on the other side of the river.

"There she is," Henry pointed as he half encouraged his son Harry toward the river and half held him safely back. "There's the *Ironsides*, she's the sturdiest boat on the lakes." That is what Henry Valentine wanted to believe. He had worked as a clerk for the Engelmann Transportation line since 1869 and although he had heard the rumors about the leaks he was firmly on the side of the company and knew that the Engelmanns were simply doing what was needed to remain competitive in the market. What he did not know, however, was the extent of the boat's leaking. Henry was also not a marine man by any stretch of the imagination. Having come from a job as a baggage master at the D&M Railroad, his job involved pointy pencils and well maintained ledgers rather than the seaworthiness of

39

Stanton Drawing of the Ironsides. *Author's Collection*

vessels. To him as well as his four year old son, the *Ironsides* was simply the queen of the fleet.

The four year old gasped in amazement at the *Ironsides* and the riverfront as a whole. It was a nest of activity as vessels of every sort seemed to move in an organized confusion of white steam and black smoke. Tugs pulled schooners and the shores of the river seemed to be a forest of masts. To the left was the Engelmann wharf and to the right of the bridge was the Goodrich dock and it was enough to fill the eyes of a little boy for quite a while. In the middle of it all, squatted the *Ironsides* with her gleaming white paint scheme. Excitedly, the Valentine family headed for the dock and the Engelmann Transportation Company's terminal. There was plenty of time as the boat was not scheduled to sail until nine o'clock that night. Still, Henry wanted to get his family securely aboard. He was not going to be making the trip across because his job required that he be at the Engelmann office on Monday morning. So he would send off his family assured in the belief that the *Ironsides* was one of the staunchest boats on the lakes. That was also the perception of the public at large. It was a hard image to argue with as the Valentine family approached the gangway to board the *Ironsides*. Her hefty wooden timbers seemed as strong as the blockhouse of a frontier fort as she sat tightly moored to the wharf. The water between her hull and the wharf was brown and filled with assorted flotsam and a bit of water spouted from a small drain in her side while white steam hissed from unseen locations. Along her boat deck were a series of four lifeboats on each side, a sight that provided assurance that in case of emergency there would more than enough boats for her passengers and crew. She appeared to be a powerful white sea monster and indeed as staunch as Henry Valentine believed.

At the home of Tim Foley, the perception of the *Ironsides* was quite different that Sunday. Tim was a young, fearless wheelsman employed aboard the *Ironsides*. He had in his mind to quit and stay ashore for the remainder of the season because of the boat's rude tendency toward leaking. When he told First Mate Crosson that he was thinking of going up the street, the mate told him not to be hasty. The company may make it worth his while to stay aboard for the rest of the season. Amazingly, the Engelmanns came across with a raise in pay for Tim if he would agree to remain aboard the *Ironsides*. Considered in the context of the era, this action alone says much about the condition of the vessel. It is almost unheard of for vessel managers in this era to offer increased wages simply to keep a wheelsman. Yet it would indeed be far cheaper to offer crewmembers another few cents a day to stay on the boat than it would be to lay the boat up and replace her bottom. In context, this indicates that the word was out around the waterfront that the *Ironsides* was "tender" and experienced mariners would have nothing to do with her. At his new rate of pay, Tim felt that he could not afford to walk the waterfront looking for another job that would pay the same. This was probably true of other members of the crew who would rather take a raise and their chances on the *Ironsides* than go looking for another job. At home, Tim expressed his opinion that the boat would not last longer than another "trip or two." His mother implored him to decline the money and stay off of the *Ironsides*, but Tim was sure that he was young enough, savvy enough and strong enough to escape and defy the lake if the vessel went down. Besides, he had just taken his boost in pay and bought a new pair of seven dollar boots, so he had to go back aboard.

Many of the boat's crew saw the regular flooding of the steamer as more of a workplace bother than a danger. One of those crewmen was Second Engineer George Cowen. To him the boat's flooding tendency and the need to constantly pump out the water was simply a disagreeable part of his job. It was all very simple, when the water gets too high in the boat you pump it out. If you get it all, then you get it all, if you don't, then you don't. It was all easier than having to go out and find another job.

It was nearly ten o'clock Sunday evening by the time that the *Ironsides* cast off her lines and departed the dock. Down on the wharf, Henry Valentine waved goodbye as his wife and son waved back. On the walk home he thought of that little sailor suited boy and he wished he could be there with him to share the adventure. Standing at rail of the drawbridge he watched the amber lights of the boat swing as the *Ironsides* made the bend and headed toward Lake Michigan. Indeed he had confidence in the Engelmann's boat. In fact he may have had more confidence in the boat than her own crew.

George Cowen was in his room napping as the *Ironsides* left Milwaukee. His shift began at one o'clock in the morning and he needed all of the rest that he could get. Shortly before the beginning of his watch, Cowen awoke to the feel of the *Ironsides* casually rolling in the seas. It was the familiar and comforting feeling of the boat being underway. As Cowen made his way into the engine room the heat of the boilers met his face while the smell of the coal and oil that made the boat come alive suddenly surrounded him. The engine room on a wooden steamer was a hard place to earn a living. Although the *Ironsides'* two steam engines were given plenty of room, this part of the boat was heavily enclosed with thick wooden walls and contained all of the heat from the steam plant. Temperatures normally hovered over the one hundred degree mark and there was precious little ventilation. In the daytime the engine room was illuminated by a huge skylight on the deckhouse roof, but in the night there were only a few oil lamps to provide light. It was a hot, steamy, smelly, dark and dangerous place to make a living, and that was exactly the way fellows such as Cowen liked it. No sooner had Cowen entered the engine room than Chief McGlue came over and met him.

"Keep a close eye on the engine George," he ordered. "I'm goin' up to get some lunch."

Cowen nodded as the chief headed up the companionway. The engine of the *Ironsides* received as little investment from the Engelmanns as the rest of the boat, but the constant attention given it by the engineers kept it running like a fine pocket watch. Nearly an hour passed before Chief McGlue returned from his meal. Cowen dutifully reported that everything was running smoothly. McGlue took a fatherly scan around the engine. He listened to it working, he felt the deck beneath his feet and the vibration of the *Ironsides* and he decided that Cowen was right, everything was working fine. Once again he left the engine room in Cowen's charge and retired to his cabin for the night.

A VOICE IN THE FOG

For the next 90 minutes the wooden deck beneath Cowen's feet rolled along in a normal manner. Then at half past three in the morning he felt the boat take on a nasty roll. The winds had turned from the southwest to the northwest and were beginning to blow a stiff gale. To the engine room crew, the weather outside was of little concern. Oilers Dan Hines, John Gilbert and Charles Wilcox spent their respective shifts moving around the steam engine and checking the assorted moving parts by placing an experienced hand upon the part. If the part felt too warm they would apply a dose of oil. This may sound like a trivial task, but without the constant attention of the oilers the engine of a steamer such as the *Ironsides* would grind itself to death in just a few hours. Down in the fire hold the rest of engine room crew, the firemen, stoked the furnaces that heated the boat's boilers. Harry Hughes, Edward Fugle and James Brown shared that duty aboard the *Ironsides*. To all of these men their world aboard the *Ironsides* consisted largely of the engine room, their cabins and the galley. Occasionally one of them would sip a cup of coffee while leaning out of the companionway and watching the lake go by, but most of their time was spent in the engine room. Actually, it did not matter if it was raining or snowing outside, the engine room never changed. It was always hot and dark and the job of keeping the boat running remained the same.

For engineers such as Cowen, there was another side to their job. The maintenance of every moving part of the *Ironsides*, from engine components to door hinges on passenger cabins, was their responsibility.

Captain Sweetman placed his full trust in his engineers and when something went wrong, he expected them to simply fix it. Onboard a vessel the engineers are also the boat's handymen. If a small problem was beginning to grow into a large problem that may go beyond the scope of the engineers abilities, the captain expected to be informed. When you mix that sort of trust with the complacency of a person such as George Cowen and add in the tendency of the *Ironsides* to leak and you have a disastrous formula.

Shortly after the winds shifted, the *Ironsides* began to corkscrew and roll in the following seas. As she rolled, her hull stretched and twisted and those countless little leaks in her bottom began to let Lake Michigan in at an alarming rate. Soon water was sloshing up through the floor grating in the engine room. Upon inspection, Cowen scoffed with a "There she goes leakin' again," attitude. Remarkably, for the next hour and a half, the water continued to intrude while Cowen shrugged off the danger. After all, the boat had taken water on nearly every passage this season, so why should tonight be any different. Finally at five o'clock in the morning, the flooding got to the point where it annoyed Cowen and he used the bilge injection pump to force it out. In spite of this token effort, the flooding grew worse. At seven o'clock in the morning, three and one half hours after the flooding had started, the water in the bottom of the *Ironsides* had risen to the point where it was knee deep in the fire hold and threatening to put out the boat's fires. The vessel had wallowed so low in the lake that the gangway doors on her sides were now vulnerable to the waves. In rapid succession the waves smashed in several of the thick wooden doors and Lake Michigan cascaded into the boat. As the waterfall of intruding doom came down the companionway stairs and burst into the engine room, Cowen decided it was time to send someone up to wake up the chief.

We can only imagine the thoughts that went through Chief McGlue's mind as he hustled down into his engine room and found if flooded with huge waves of filthy water sloshing from side to side as the *Ironsides* rolled. Cowen and other members of the engine room crew were franticly working the pumps in a pointless effort. One quick glance told him all that he needed to know, the *Ironsides* was doomed. Minutes later the Chief was up in the pilothouse where Captain Sweetman was desperately trying to turn the boat around and put her head to the wind. The *Ironsides*, however, was hung up in the trough of the seas and not able to come around. Chief McGlue told the captain that he would go back down into the engine room and try backing one engine while running the other forward in the hope of pulling the boat out of the sea trough.

Down in the cargo hold, Tim Foley was working with his shipmates in a desperate battle to keep the lake out. They were using hand pumps to expel the water, but each wave brought in ten times more water than they could pump out. Shortly before nine o'clock the captain came down and mustered Tim and another crewman to help him raise the *Ironsides'* sail. He calculated that it would give them a couple of miles per hour toward the Grand Haven shore. Once the sail was up Captain Sweetman ordered Foley up to the pilothouse to "try to keep her in trim" with the wheel. Just then there was the sound of a volcano rumble and from every doorway that lead to the lower parts of the boat huge billows of steam erupted. Moments later there was shouting as the men of the engine crew came scrambling up. The water had put the boat's fires out and now she was powerless. Foley stopped on his way to the pilothouse and took off his new boots. He figured he was in for some swimming and they would only weigh him down.

"There goes seven dollars." He said as he tossed the new boots overboard.

Then he reached into his pocket and pulled out his knife. Using the knife he cut both of his pants legs off at the knees to make for easier swimming, then he headed up to the pilothouse. The wind was not gusting, but was instead blowing in a constant howl. In the confines of the bird cage pilothouse of the *Ironsides*, Tim Foley found it hard to maintain any sense of safety. It was clear to him that the boat was going down and the only real question was when she would take her dive. The seas were later described by acting Purser Norman Watkins as being "Two blocks wide at the base and in order to see the crests you had to look up at an angle of 70 degrees." You do not have to be good at math to figure out that this is a wild exaggeration. If you sit down and actually draw it out, using a common city block being 100 yards or 300-feet long, multiply that by two and then project a 70 degree angle from each end of that 600-foot base, they meet at a wave crest of just over 780-feet tall. That is about 20 times taller than the largest waves ever found on

A VOICE IN THE FOG

Lake Michigan. Considering the time of the year, and the normal weather patterns, it is likely that the *Ironsides* was in seas that were 12 to 18-feet at their worst. To Tim Foley it all made little difference. He was sure that he could out wit Lake Michigan. For that reason he took the boat's wheel and held it as steady as he could, just as Captain Sweetman had ordered.

Some witnesses ashore initially claimed that the *Ironsides* had attempted an approach to the harbor, but then turned back out into the lake. From the recorded accounts of the crew of the vessel, it appears that the *Ironsides* never was able to make such a maneuver. It is likely that what the witnesses ashore saw was the boat being spun about into the sea trough and they interpreted that as a turn. Although Foley held the vessel's wheel until she sank, he really had no effect on her course. There was no water passing over the rudder and so his hands on the wheel did nothing more than obey Captain Sweetman's orders.

Once the fires were out and the boilers could no longer make steam, and the *Ironsides* was flooded to the point where waves were freely boarding through her smashed gangways, the decision was made to alert the passengers. As Purser Watkins went around pounding his fist on each stateroom door the occupants were already well aware that they were on a sinking ship. Still, Watkins dutifully went to each cabin and told everyone to go to the lifeboats. Unlike most passenger vessels of this era, the *Ironsides* carried more than enough lifeboats for everyone onboard and so there would be no trouble in deciding who would go or who would stay. No such thing as a

Lifeboats depart the floundering Ironsides.
Author's Collection

"lifeboat drill" was required or conducted aboard vessels of this era, however, and so there were no assigned lifeboat stations or procedures. Everyone was simply expected to find a boat with enough room left in it and get aboard. Then hope that the sailors manning the boat actually knew how to operate the rig.

Lifeboats from the *Ironsides* were lowered into the water first and then released from the davits. Passengers were loaded at the gangways and each boat was placed in the charge of a crewmember. The first boat to be loaded was placed under the command of Henry Hazelbarth who was the first mate on the steamer *City Of Toledo*. That vessel was currently operating in the Engelmann fleet and he was on his way to meet her and sail her back to Milwaukee. He had made the dreadful mistake of bringing his wife along on this trip, the result being that now he was helping her into a lifeboat. After Mrs. Hazelbarth was safely seated, the little Valentine Boy was handed into her outstretched arms and seated. His mother followed and then both ladies hovered together to shelter the little boy. No one kept track of the number of passengers and crew who boarded this boat, but Sam Watkins, kin to the *Ironsides'* purser got in last and the lifeboat shoved off. At that same moment two other lifeboats were being loaded. One of the boats was in the charge of Purser Norm Watkins and contained nine passengers. The other boat was placed in the charge of the ship's porter, Peter Riley and contained the ship's chambermaid, Maggie Young and eight passengers. Both of these boats got away from the *Ironsides* at about the same time and headed for shore. The fourth lifeboat was placed in the charge of Second Mate A.B. Pitman. A gaggle of crew, including Second Engineer Cowen, clamored aboard and the boat shoved off.

While Cowen's boat moved away from the *Ironsides*, the big steamer began rapidly sinking. They looked back and saw that First Mate Crosson had climbed the rigging of the foremast and was waving farewells toward the departing lifeboats. In a moment the whole wreck lurched and sank beneath him. The mast on which he had been sitting snapped above him and swung down swatting him from the rigging like a golf club. Amazingly the steamer's hurricane deck remained on the surface. It is likely that this deck had broken away from the lower hull and was now left floating. This was fortunate for Cowen and the rest of the crew in his boat, because shortly after they departed the sinking *Ironsides*, their lifeboat capsized.

They lost most of their oars and when they righted the lifeboat they had nothing to bail her out. Swimming as best they could, the crew of this lifeboat managed to drag it back to the wreck. Now the hurricane deck provided a temporary island upon which timid feet with soggy socks splashed about as the castaways went seeking provisions. They managed to scavenge some oars and a few buckets with which to bail and then returned to their lifeboat. Quickly she was rid of most of the water as they rowed away from the wreck. The men stopped long enough to pluck a battered Crosson from the lake and pull him to safety.

The last lifeboat to leave the *Ironsides* contained Captain Sweetman, Chief McGlue and Tim Foley. In all, five lifeboats and all of the passengers and crew were able to get away from the sinking *Ironsides*. Now they had a dangerous four mile journey to escape Lake Michigan. Second Engineer Cowen and his fellow castaways managed to fully free their lifeboat of water and slid smoothly into Grand Haven harbor. On a nearby beach north of Grand Haven the bow of the lifeboat under the care of ship's porter Peter Riley skidded into the sand as a breaking wave slammed into its stern. He had lost two occupants overboard on the way in. Charles Wimmel, who was a passenger, was washed out by a wave and consumed by Lake Michigan. One of the ship's cooks, whose name is recorded as both "Dundasher" and "Dundas" was also washed from the lifeboat. He managed to swim over a mile to shore and survived. The lifeboat that was being managed by Purser Watkins got to within a half mile of the beach when Lake Michigan reached out and flipped it over. Everyone in the boat was flung into the water, yet all of them made it back to the lifeboat. They all clung to their turtled lifeboat until they were washed ashore and pulled from the lake by local residents.

Ed Killian, who ran the "Milwaukee House" in Grand Haven immediately opened his doors to the survivors. In fact, the entire town of Grand Haven came to the aid of the castaways. Hundreds of people lined the beaches and the men in town who were the strongest swimmers were poised to dive into the surf and recover both the living and the dead. Unfortunately, after Norman Watkins' overturned lifeboat and the nine people who were clinging to it were dragged to safety, all that remained for the swimmers to recover were dead bodies. Somewhere between the wreck and the beach, Captain Sweetman's lifeboat had been overturned by Lake Michigan and all aboard it were drown. That toll included Tim Foley whose youthful self image of being able to escape, no matter what the lake tried to do to him, had proven to be terribly wrong. Also capsized by the lake was the lifeboat under the command of Henry Hazelbarth. As the first mate on the *City Of Toledo*, he was considered to be an extremely competent sailor and well able to handle the lifeboat under any circumstances. Still, Lake Michigan got the better of him and tossed his lifeboat over, dumping its human cargo into the icy water. Out of all of those who occupied the lifeboat, only Sam Watkins managed to swim the one and one half mile distance to shore. This was his second brush with Lake Michigan in just three months. He had been out on the lake on the sloop

Lake Breeze on the fourth of July when a powerful squall came past. The boat was turtled and Sam had to cling to its overturned hull and wait until another vessel came by and rescued him and the other man who had been aboard. Now he had survived a second attempt by Lake Michigan to take his life.

Through the day the lake continued to deposit bodies onto the beach north of Grand Haven. During that time the body of Nattie Valentine was pulled from the surf by local residents. After some searching of the beach, the body of little Harry Valentine, Nattie's four year old son, dressed in his blue sailor's suit, was found half buried in the sand. A day later a dozen of the bodies from the *Ironsides* were returned to Milwaukee in plain pine boxes aboard the Engelmann steamer *Saginaw*. In a scene of sorrow the next of kin met the boxes at the Engelmann's dock and warehouse. Henry Valentine came to identify and claim his wife and little boy. Looking at the little sailor, the grieving father wondered "Why?"

Survivors who worked for Engelmann Transportation gave self serving statements to the press wherein they flatly denied that the *Ironsides* had ever leaked. The most unconvincing of these came from Second Engineer Cowen who denied that the boat had ever leaked, but later stated that the water was coming in "from the bottom" of the boat. Such statements make sense when you consider that when the *Ironsides* went down, these folks were suddenly all unemployed. There would be little hope that Engelmann Transportation would hire them back if they had told the press that the *Ironsides* was a leaking tub.

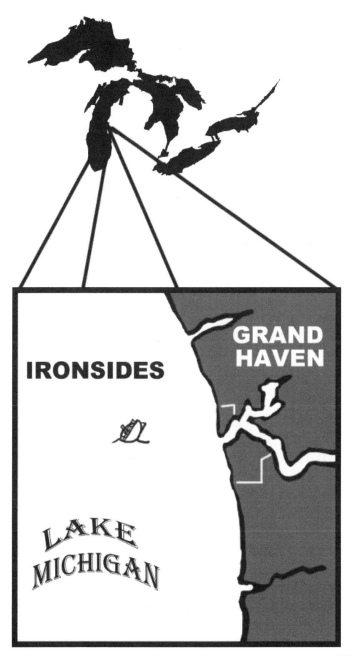

Of course a blue ribbon panel of vessel owners and local politicians was assembled in Grand Haven to investigate the sinking of the *Ironsides*. Although other steamers of the same size, construction and age were out on Lake Michigan in that same weather, and all of them got into their docks without wetting one piece of their cargo, the investigators said that there was no evidence to show that the *Ironsides* was in a leaking or otherwise unseaworthy condition. The wet cargoes that remained on the docks at both Grand Haven and Milwaukee were advantageously overlooked and the accounts of those who thought they had witnessed the *Ironsides* make a turn away from Grand Haven were considered. The blame was put onto Captain Sweetman for turning his boat away from a safe port and heading her into the storm where the waves then pounded her until she sank. The fact that the surviving engineer had stated that Chief McGlue reversed one engine and went forward on the other, but they still could not get the boat to turn from the sea trough was also overlooked. Since both Captain Sweetman and Chief McGlue were dead, it was somewhat hard for them to testify. So it was that the captain of the *Ironsides* was blamed for the sinking because he was said to have made a turn that he could never have performed. The Engelmanns were, naturally, cleared of all blame by their peers.

Without doubt, each time that Henry Valentine looked out across Lake Michigan he envisioned his wife and son. He felt the pain of their loss and wondered about their last minutes on the lake. We too can look toward the lake and wonder about that little boy in the sailor's suit bobbing in the huge waves after being thrown from the *Ironsides*' lifeboat. How many times did little Harry Valentine's voice call out for "Help!" and is it still being heard today?

One last haunting twist to this story occurred to the author in the summer of 2003. While crossing Lake Michigan aboard the ferry boat *Badger.* I was on my way to Oshkosh, Wisconsin with my wife. We had taken the late evening ferry which left Ludington at eight o'clock and was due into Manitowoc at midnight. A hefty southwest wind was blowing that evening and once out on the lake the *Badger* was taking eight to 12-foot seas and rolling comfortably. For many of the passengers the sight of Lake Michigan's chop and the sound of the spray was an awesome sight. A few passengers retreated to the interior of the boat in fear, and a few others found themselves stricken with seasickness. Most of the folks, however, held faith in the *Badger* and her crew and simply rode out the trip with a good book or rocked to sleep in an available seat. My wife and I spent a lot of time out on deck enjoying the summer winds and pure beauty of the lake. As we sat out on a bench in the growing evening darkness I could not help but think of the vessels and people gone by in the history that I so often study and research. I pondered at length the *Ironsides* and her people. Nearby the door to the lounge opened, and out onto the rolling deck stepped a little girl. Boldly she stepped up to the rail and looked directly over the side toward the heaving lake. Standing on tiptoes she studied the waves and depths. Then she turned toward us and brushed her golden hair from her angelic little face.

"Where are you going?" she asked.

"We're going that way." I replied pointing toward the west.

"I'm going to my cousin's house in Wisconsin." She went on without a bit of reservation. "We're going to play and have fun for a whole week. What's your name?"

"My name is Wes and this is my wife Teresa."

Placing her hands on her hips the little sprite of the lakes lifted her chin. "My name's Nattolie."

A moment later the door to the lounge opened and the voice of a family member called, "Nattie, get back in here." With that the little girl turned and marched back into the lounge area to rejoin her family. Although the ghosts of the past may haunt the average person, their names alone can haunt the research historian. Such was the case on a choppy night on Lake Michigan and an angel of the lake with no fear of the winds and waves.

THE GHOST LANTERN

Patrick O'Mally, a reporter from the *Detroit Post* newspaper, arrived in the tiny town of Harrisville, Michigan on an excursion up the shore in search of interesting news tidbits. It was late August of 1884 and he was enjoying those last few days of summer on the Lake Huron coast and largely using news snooping as an excuse to do so. In this era, Harrisville was a fishing town in the summer and a lumber town in the winter. During the fall and spring it was mostly a mud hole. Poking about in town O'Mally happened upon an old fisherman and engaged him in conversation. Somehow the talk came around to local legends and the leathery skinned fisherman started talking about the haunting of a local shipwreck. O'Mally confessed that he had never heard of the story and the fisherman invited him out that night to witness the ghost firsthand. Following dinner the reporter gained a room at a local boarding house and waited for the coming of night. The fisherman had been very specific that O'Mally should meet him at the dock at exactly 11:45 in the evening. As darkness fell, the town of

Harrisville drifted off to sleep and by the time that the reporter's pocket watch indicated that he should head down toward the dock, the night had grown deathly silent. Walking down the road his footsteps did not echo, but seemed to be soaked up by the night, like a black sponge. Although the evening was warm, a shiver ran down O'Mally's spine–he felt sure that dozens of eyes were watching him. His growing case of the creeps would soon grow much worse.

This story has its roots in economic events that developed in the two decades prior to O'Mally's visit to Harrisville. In the years following the civil war the lumbering industry in the region of the Great Lakes went from a booming growth to an explosive growth. Along with that growth came a parallel growth in the population of the territory. Small lumber towns such as Alpena, Michigan suddenly became cities as new residents flowed in and settled. Of course, all of these folks needed transportation and that was best accommodated by way of the lakes. Upon the surface of these freshwater highways, dozens of steamboats and hundreds of sailing vessels moved people and products. By the end of the 1870s the most efficient way to travel in the region of the Great Lakes was by water.

Passenger steamers of this era were somewhat of a cross between the "Palace Steamers" of the early 1860s and the utilitarian "break-bulkers" that were the delivery vans of the lakes. The Palace Steamers were equipped with all of the luxuries of the finest hotels that could be found ashore, while a break-bulker was much more like a roadside motel placed upon the back of a package freighter. When it was found that the Palace

steamers were too expensive to operate and still gain maximum profit, the vessel barons often pulled out of the passenger business and simply abandoned their boats to rot in the backwaters. This left a void in the transportation business that up-start vesselmen were willing to fill by investing in a cheap boat and fitting it out with comfortable accommodations that were less palatial but still had a large dose of fancy. The compliment of passengers who booked passage aboard these steamers closely mirrored the American melting pot. Walking their decks could be found people from every sort of background on their way to every sort of future. From trappers and lumberjacks to bankers and lumber barons, they all found passage aboard these steamers to be to their liking. Such vessels were staffed with as many as 50 crewmembers and the boats themselves were worked as hard as their equipment could bear. This was an era before government inspection of hulls and a time when only a boat's boilers were required to be inspected. Even in the area of boiler inspections, actual visits to a boat by an inspector were so rare that most steamers were never visited and corruption and bribery were commonplace. Yet the owners knew that the passengers were concerned only with a punctual arrival and good meals. So long as the boat did not sink from under them, the passengers would pay their fare and probably return for another voyage.

Among the fleet of vessels providing access to the boomtowns of the lumber industry was the sidewheel steamer *Marine City*. Built in her namesake city by Thomas Arnold over the summer of 1866 she was launched as a barge in the fall of that same year. Her first enrollment was issued in Detroit on October 19, 1866 but there is doubt as to if she ever operated as a barge, other than being towed to Detroit where she was immediately converted to a sidewheel passenger steamer. Constructed of wood, the *Marine City* measured 192-feet long, 27.75-feet in beam and 10.66-feet in depth and as a steamer she had a gross tonnage of 695.89. She went to work in the spring of 1867 hauling passengers and cargo from Detroit to points along Michigan's lower peninsula. Cities such as Saginaw, Tawas, Oscoda, Alcona, Alpena and Mackinaw were her usual stops.

For many years following her introduction to the passenger trade, the *Marine City* was a common sight along the waterways associated with Lake Huron. In her career the boat had plenty of adventures. While groping her way through a spring fog in June of 1872 the *Marine City* ran ashore near Bark Shanty. After being lightered she was floated again and went on her way. In the summer of 1873 she was host to an expedition that set out to lay the first submarine telegraph cable across the Straits of Mackinaw. When the expedition arrived, however, they discovered that the bottom of the straits was far deeper and much more rough than they had anticipated. The Straits of Mackinaw are, in fact, made up of a prehistoric

The sidewheel steamer Marine City. *Author's Collection*

riverbed and canyon and the flimsy cable that the expedition had brought with them would never stand the stress of being strung across the expanse of an undersea canyon. The party set out to find a smoother bottom on which to plant their telegraph cable. When they did find a suitable bottom, they also found that the amount of cable they had brought was about a mile to short and the expedition was postponed indefinitely. Also in 1873 the *Marine City* was sold from the Shore Line to the management of Mr. D. Gallagher. Even with the change in management the *Marine City's* routes stayed about the same and her adventures continued.

On Sunday evening, April 19, 1874 the *Marine City* was on her way down from Alpena to Detroit and nearly in the middle of Lake Huron. A fierce spring gale was blowing and the boat was rolling in the seas. Many of the passengers aboard were groaning with seasickness, but one passenger, Mrs. Dust was groaning for a very different reason. Having boarded in Alpena, she was nine months pregnant and the pain of labor had chosen this moment in time to come calling. With the help of one of the boat's stewards, John McKinloch, Mrs. Dust gave birth to a baby boy aboard the *Marine City* in the middle of a gale. Of course, there are far more stories such as these whose setting was the decks of the *Marine City*. Such were the ways of a working passenger boat in the mid 1800s.

Aboard the *Marine City* during the 1880 sailing season, the duty of keeping the passengers satisfied with good food fell to Chief Cook James Griffin, but the world of the boat's dining room was under the supreme command of headwaiter Richard Schultz. The story

THE GHOST LANTERN

goes that once the day's final meal had been served, Schultz would have his stewards clean the dining room and reset it in preparation for the next morning's breakfast. It was a process that went on until late in the evening as every crumb had to be removed from the carpet and the entire space made spotlessly clean. Each napkin and every glass had to be placed in exactly the proper position in preparation for the upcoming morning meal. Schultz was a fanatic when it came to his dining room and from its place setting to its rules for seating he left absolutely no margin. A good example of this took place back in 1877 when the *Marine City* made a trip to Alpena with Mr. A.W. Comstock, an ego bloated Alpena banker, and his family aboard. The dining room rules were that adults were to eat at the first table and children at the second table. Banker Comstock insisted that his children would eat at the first table and his over-blown self-image came head to head with Shultz's authority. The two men argued and "a scuffle ensued." Unfortunately for Banker Comstock, when the boat arrived at Detroit he found out that aboard the *Marine City*, Shultz was the final authority in the dining room. Comstock was arrested as the boat docked and ended up paying a 25 dollar fine. The Comstock children never did dine at the first table. Shultz was just as hard nosed when it came to the preparation of his dining room. He would visit the darkened dining room every night at midnight, lantern in hand, and inspect every inch of it to make sure that his stewards had set everything properly. As he walked quietly around the tables, the amber light of his oil lantern reflected among the glasses and illuminated the dishware. Each item was examined for cleanliness and Schultz's eyes could easily find the slightest hint of contaminant. Even if he simply suspected that a dish or saucer may be soiled he would snatch the plate from the setting and examine it more closely. The thick china plates were engraved on the back with a green decoration that included a unicorn and they not only had to be free of soiling but also unchipped. Schultz's inspections were insanely meticulous and he was obsessive in conducting them. Pity the poor stewards who had left anything out of order as Schultz would come pounding on their cabin door and insure that they lost plenty of sleep as they reset the entire room–this time under his glaring supervision and by the light of his lantern.

August 28, 1880 was a fine sunny, summer day and mid-afternoon found the *Marine City* sailing routinely out of Thunder Bay and the city of Alpena. Sources conflict as to her actual destination on the lower lakes. Some say Detroit while others say Toledo and some even say she was headed for Toronto. With certainty we can say that one of the boat's destinations was Detroit but she was scheduled to make an intermediate stop in the little town of Alcona just a short distance south of Alpena before heading down Lake Huron. As the boat was making the dock at Alcona, several dock whollopers stood ready to load aboard the cargo that was waiting. Mostly the cargo consisted of wood shingles with a few other items that would be placed in her hold. Strong men with strong backs would be the method by which the boat was loaded with cargo, but another form of cargo, would be self loading–that was the *Marine City's* passengers. Records show that eight paying passengers boarded the boat at Alcona. But when the *Marine City* departed the dock, she had two extra passengers aboard. Among the dock workers who had been hired to man-handle the cargo, there were three individuals who cared not about the day's pay, but rather were interested in the *Marine City* herself. These roustabouts had spent their summer on the lakeshore and were now looking for a free ride down to Detroit. As they loaded the cargo, they also found a good location to stow away.

Swiftly the cargo was loaded and the *Marine City* departed the Alcona dock with her passengers and stowaways. No records exist to tell us how many passengers she actually had aboard, but the best counts say that she had more than 100 passengers and a crew of 40. It was a healthy paying load and about her average burden. Most folks ashore paid about as much attention to the *Marine City's* departure as any modern person would the departure of a bus. As soon as her doors were closed the residents of Alcona went back to their everyday business. Captain Comer left the command of the boat in the hands of First Mate William Smith. The good captain knew that he would be navigating down the St. Clair and Detroit rivers through the night and he always took a protracted nap as the boat headed across the open lake.

Down in the boat's cargo hold, the stowaways were relaxing and looking forward to a leisurely and free ride down the lake. Up in the dining room, Schultz was putting the final preparations in place for another perfect supper. In the galley, Chief Cook Griffin was making sure that there would be plenty of food and the quality would be suitable for Schultz's dining room as the smell of wonderful dinner delights hovered around the boat. Surely the aroma from the galley would attract the passengers long before Schultz could ring the dinner bell. Suddenly, however, those tasty aromas were mixed with a pungent and vile stench. Passengers began to lift their noses and soon the whisper was heard all around the boat, "something's burning!"

Over her career the *Marine City* had spent many a season hauling large numbers of passengers and tons of freight with great success. She had also spent 14 long winters sitting idle and waiting to return to activity in the spring. Normally her engine and boiler received most of the refit attention and occasionally her hull got a new plank or two. Her superstructure, which consisted of her cabins and upper decks got little more than a fresh coat of paint each season. So, by 1880 her wood framing was as tender as kindling wood. Although there is no record as to where the fire began, it would be a moot point anyhow. The fact is, that in a matter of minutes, the entire mid section of the vessel was burning like haystack.

A burning vessel's captain has one option in cases such as the *Marine City's* and that is to turn his boat toward the nearest land and attempt to beach her. The best estimate is the *Marine City* was about five miles from Alcona when the fire erupted. In a matter of minutes her upper works were an inferno and her captain had her turned and headed back toward shore. It was already too late. The *Marine City* was rapidly consuming itself and at its top speed of just over 12 miles per hour there was no way that it could reach land and be beached.

Since the fire had started amidship, one of the first components of the boat to be consumed were her lifeboats. For the passengers there were few life jackets–if any. So the prospect of being burned alive soon forced the passengers to select their only option–jumping overboard. The only problem with that was that along with the boat's lifeboats, the boat's engine controls were also amidships and had been abandoned to the flames in the "full ahead" position. All 100 plus passengers were gathered on the boat's bow and if any of them were to go over the side, they would be sucked into the *Marine City's* huge paddle wheels. Their only choice was to hope that the engine became disabled by the flames before the fire reached the bow. Engines and boilers are made of steel and iron and are far more resistant to fire than are human bodies and it became clear that the boat would not stop because of her burning hull.

Ashore at Alcona the locals saw the smoke and flames long before the *Marine City* had turned to run back. They assembled in a rag-tag rescue fleet and headed out in anything that resembled a boat. They knew that the passengers and crew of the *Marine City* would soon be in the water and the result could be a huge death toll. It is important to keep in mind that in this era, most folks could not swim. In fact, may who made their living working out on the lake could not swim. Organized swimming classes and the social effort to teach swimming were not implemented until the early 1900s, so for many of the people aboard the *Marine City,* the prospect of jumping into the water was just as deadly as that of being burned alive.

No record is left to us as to how the *Marine City* found her final resting place. If she hit a shallow spot and grounded or if she had her sea cocks opened and was scuttled or if her engine works finally did give out, we do not know. It is easy to speculate, however, that having started below decks the fire had enough time to burn through her lower hull and open her to the lake. The means mattered little as the boat finally came to a halt just over two miles out of Alcona and her passengers began grabbing anything that may float and jumping overboard. By the time that help arrived the crowd of passengers were mostly in the water. The tug *Vulcan* came alongside the burning wreck and started taking survivors. The fire was so hot that it set the tug on fire several times and her crew fought to extinguish the sprouting flames. By the time the *Vulcan* pulled away she was badly scorched. Soon the *Marine City* was nothing more than a smoldering heap, most of which was resting on the sandy bottom of Lake Huron.

Through simple courage the residents of Alcona managed to save all but nine of the *Marine City's* people. Among those lost were two of the three stowaways, Head Cook Griffin and most prominently Richard Schultz, who died along with his treasured dining room.

THE GHOST LANTERN

Protruding several feet above the water, the bones of the *Marine City* remained visible until the 1950s. It was in August of 1881, however, that a strange phenomena began to take place out at the wreck. It was this event that the old fisherman had offered to show to Patrick O'Mally four years after the loss of the boat. As O'Mally arrived at the dock he found the fisherman waiting for him.

"So ya' wanna' see it do ya'?" the old net spreader chided.

"Sure," O'Mally retorted, "show me yer' willow-the-wisp."

"Like I told ya', it comes out right at midnight on the button."

The two men stood silently and waited several minutes until O'Mally's pocket watch read exactly midnight.

"That's 12 o'clock." O'Mally sneered as he slipped the timepiece back into his pocket.

"Yep," the fisherman snorted as he pointed out onto the open lake, "and there she is."

O'Mally squinted in the direction that the fisherman was pointing and sure enough he saw a dim green light had appeared far out on the lake. The light appeared to float just above the surface as if carried by an unseen hand.

"Let's get a boat!" the reporter whispered excitedly.

"We can go out there but you ain't gonna find nothin' but the wreck of the old *Marine City*." The fisherman explained. "That light sits out there and hovers over her grave every night in the month of August, then it's gone 'til next year."

Still, O'Mally insisted and soon the two men were heading out into the lake in a small rowboat. O'Mally pulled hard at the oars and made sure to feather the blades between each stroke so as to remain silent. At the same time he kept looking over his shoulder to see if the light was still there.

"You keep pullin' at them oars like that and yer' gonna lame yerself." The fisherman warned. "You can't sneak up on it, we've tried. The darned thing knows yer' comin.'"

Sure enough as they neared the wreck the light began to drift away as if whoever was holding it was walking off. O'Mally could easily see that there was no other boat out there. Even if there was a boat it could not have remained afloat over the wreckage. There was only the light hovering and O'Mally had the distinct impression that someone was carrying it. Yet the light drifted away across the lake and as the two men arrived at the wreck the light simply vanished. O'Mally was stunned and when he looked back at the old fisherman he saw him smiling.

"That a good enough story for ya'?" the fisherman asked.

O'Mally was speechless and puzzled. "What do ya' think it is?" he asked the fisherman.

"Who knows," the old man pondered, "probably someone lost with this wreck who still has some business here."

Perhaps the old fisherman was right. Perhaps that lantern from beyond that appeared every night in August was held by that hard nosed and obsessive head waiter. Maybe every night in August, Schultz returned and inspected a dining room that he would not let die. In reading this story you may ask the question as to if the light still haunts the wreck site. My answer is that I do not know–I never had the nerve to go and find out. Perhaps Schultz's dining room is best left alone and in his care forever.

ARCHIE'S STEPS

Some ghost stories are nearly as hard to capture as the ghosts themselves. Often it takes a great deal of hunting and the repeated asking of a single silly-sounding favor, "Tell me about the ghost of…" Usually the people asked to tell such a rare tale have no idea how to fulfill the request. Sometimes, however, they can refer you to someone else who has a bit or a piece to add to a story that was handed down from one generation to another over the years. Often the details are conflicting and the basis of the yarn is obscured. Such is the yarn of the ghost of the Raspberry Island lighthouse.

It was just before America's entry into World War II and Anna and her cousin Mary were just children growing up on a farm. Although the farm itself was a short distance from the harbor city of Ashland, Wisconsin, the little girls rarely got the chance to travel into town or to see the lake. Any such trips were special adventures for the girls, so when the opportunity came up to go all the way out to the Raspberry Island lighthouse their excitement nearly boiled over. Neither of the little girls really knew exactly where Raspberry Island was, but in their minds it was a far away and exotic place. Just the term "island" brought to mind images of palm trees, sandy beaches and grass huts. The night before their departure both Anna and Mary hardly slept a wink. They simply laid awake and exchanged fantasies about what it would be like to go to the island and live there for three whole days.

Following that chatter filled night, the two little girls began the day with an energy level that only children can muster after a sleepless eve. With their bags stowed in the car they began their adventure out to Raspberry Island. They had planned every step as if they were actually in control and knew what to expect. Of course their trip was actually under the control of their adult kin and what they could never have expected was an upcoming encounter with a ghost named Archie.

Just the trip to nearby Ashland itself was an adventure. As they rolled off of the dirt road that led

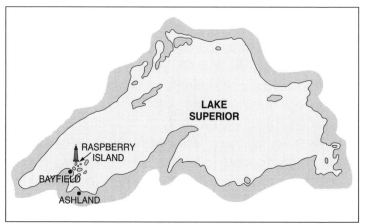

from the countryside and onto the highway that ran through the city, the waters of Lake Superior glistened in front of Anna and Mary. Soon one of the adults drew their attention,

"Look kids!" Anna's mom beckoned, "Look at the big ore dock!"

There was just enough time to catch a glimpse of the dark giant as the car rolled past the dock, then as they rounded the corner the girls could see the long brown dock as it extended out into the water. Next to the dock and dwarfed by its size was one of the big oreboats. No sooner had the first been passed than there were two more. Anna and Mary gazed in delight as their car passed under the huge trestle. The city of Ashland had more huge stone buildings than anyplace they had ever seen before and more cars and people than they would see in a whole summer. It seemed to be a bustling metropolis to the two girls from the Wisconsin farmland.

As the family car left the highway and turned on the dirt road to Bayfield the trees seemed to swallow it whole. Almost as if traveling down a dark quiet tree tunnel, Anna and Mary watched as an isolated green forest passed. The only breaks were occasional farms, as the trip now became long and lack of sleep from the previous night soon took its toll on the two girls. They awoke when the car stopped and both peered out the window at the town of Bayfield.

Bayfield, Wisconsin was, in the years prior to World War II, a far cry from the tourist jewel of the Great Lakes that it is today. To Anna and Mary it was a jumble of wood frame buildings and fishing nets and boats. To them it did not look at all like a place where they would want to stop and get out of the car. Anna's dad had gone into one of the nasty looking doorways and in a minute he returned saying that someone was waiting for them down by a dock. With a jam of a gear and the whine of reverse, he backed the car a bit and wheeled around toward a new direction. This time the car bumped along as Mary's uncle zigzagged in among the boats and nets. Again he got out and walked away among the jumble. Soon he returned, opened the trunk and began to remove the few bags of luggage that the family had packed.

"Come on." He prodded through the window, "let's get goin' they're ready."

It was at this point that the two girls realized that neither of them had considered exactly what sort of a boat would take them out to the island. When the two girls thought of a boat, they both envisioned something like an ocean liner—such would not be the case. They walked shyly along the dock which seemed as if it were about to collapse under their feet. Everywhere was the smell of fish and the water seemed green and very deep. Big rocks covered with fuzzy green stuff were all over the bottom and occasionally a piece of something man-made could be seen sunken here and there. Off to one side there were a couple of old half-sunken vessels that had been left to rot. It was hardly the sort of place that a little girl imagined as fun to begin an island adventure. When they reached the boat that was to take them out to the island, the two little girls were appalled to see what they would be riding on, or more aptly—riding "in." It was a fishing tug and was enclosed with only a small sliding door through which the girls could enter. It was weather beaten and appeared as if it would sink at any moment. While Anna and Mary contemplated the boat, Anna's father was greeted by a man who was introduced to the girls simply as "the Captain." He was dark and leathery, showing too many hours spent in the sun on the open lake. He had far too few teeth and a gruff and scraggly manner–to the two little girls he was a pirate, they just knew it. The big ugly, smelly captain hardly growled at the little girls as they were loaded aboard like so many pounds of fish. The smell was repulsive and everywhere there were fish scales and assorted nasty looking things. Life on the farm was never squeaky clean and animal refuse and other assorted messy stuff was common, both girls were not shy about getting their hands dirty–but this was different. Just finding an acceptable place to sit was troublesome.

The inside of a fish tug that once roamed the waters of Bayfield. Author's Collection

The inside of a fishing tug. Author's Collection

As the fishing boat left the dock there was a clamor of machinery powering the boat and water hitting the hull. Through the little hatchway the girls could see the distant shorelines and assorted sailboats rocking in the distance. In a cruise that seemed to last for a week the boat made its way up along the west channel of the Apostle Islands. Soon the fishing tug slowed and rocked and appeared to be maneuvering. Then came a series of "thumps" and the fishing boat suddenly stopped rocking–they were at the dock. It took little more than a wave of a hand to coax the two little girls out of the smelly fishing tug and into the bright sunshine and fresh Lake Superior breeze.

In modern times, no one really recalls how or why Anna and Mary's family had been invited to stay at the lighthouse. Apparently someone knew someone and someone invited someone to come out for a few days.

The result was that the two girls and their adult kin met a friendly Coast Guardsman and were welcomed as guests at Raspberry Island. Stepping onto the dock Anna and Mary looked up and beheld the most beautiful thing that they had ever seen. Way up atop the bluff was the Raspberry Island lighthouse. A long steep stairway lead from the dock to the lighthouse grounds and the girls could hardly contain themselves from dashing up to the lighthouse. Anna's mother kept control as long as she could, but before long the two little girls were on their way up the stairs and toward their adventure.

Raspberry Island was nothing like either Anna or Mary had imagined. There were no palm trees or tropical birds. The island was covered with thick old-growth forest with the only clear area being the lighthouse grounds. Still, there was plenty of room for

Raspberry Island Lighthouse. Author's Collection

running and playing on the grounds. The lighthouse itself is actually three apartments in a single building. Established in the later half of the 1860s, one side of the dwelling is the keeper's quarters while the other side is divided into the assistant keeper's quarters on the lower floor and the second assistant keeper's quarters on the upper floor. The light tower itself is integrated into the middle of the structure. To Anna and Mary it made little difference how the lighthouse was laid out. To them it was a fairy tale castle on top of the world.

Following a full day of play and a wonderful dinner, the lighthouse staff and their guests gathered in the family room. It was then that the sound of footsteps was heard by everyone. The sound was that of heavy boots walking up the stairway that led from the first floor to the second floor bedrooms. These were not quiet distant steps, but rather were clear resounding

Archie's stairway. Author's Collection

footsteps on the stairs. For a long moment the room was silent. Then Mary got up and peeked around the corner and up the stairs.

"Who's there?" she asked.

"Oh, you won't find anyone little lady." One of the Coast Guardsmen remarked casually. "That's just old Archie."

"Who's Archie?" Anna's mother asked.

Like campers around a fire the entire family sat and learned the tale of the spirit that haunts the stairway. Together they discovered that this lighthouse upon the bluff came into Coast Guard possession with a story of love and murder attached.

Obscure legend has it that there once was a local boy named Archie who had followed his father's career path and become a fisherman. The time was just following the end of the Civil War and shortly after the Raspberry Island lighthouse had been constructed. Archie was just a teenager when his affections were captured by a local girl named Margie. Margie was kin to a local lumber broker and of a quite well-to-do breeding. She wanted little to do with the bumbling teenage boy who always came romping toward her like a big dumb dog. Her sights were set on places far from Bayfield and sophistication that was over and above the romantic crush of a local fisherboy. Still, no matter how many times she scoffed at him and no matter how she rebuffed his affections, Archie kept coming around for more. It got to the point where his interest in Margie became a real annoyance for the lumber debutant. At one point she told him directly that if he wanted to gain the attention of any lady of status, he had better make something of himself other than a smelly fisherman. Most lads would have been put off by such a remark, but not Archie. He considered it to be advice on how to gain Margie's attention and thus became determined to "make better of himself." After some hard consideration he devised the perfect plan.

In those early days of the U.S. Lighthouse Board, gaining a position as a keeper or assistant keeper of the light was sometimes more a matter of what political party you belonged to rather than what types of qualifications you had. The selection of keepers and hiring of assistants was often in the control of local political leaders rather than any formal Federal hiring process. In the mid-1880s there was a huge shake-up in the staffing of lighthouses, the Lighthouse Board went through a series of reforms to shake loose those political favors and gain a more even-handed approach to hiring. In Archie's time however, the lighthouses in the Apostle Islands were under the control of a local political party that just happened to be the same one that got his father's votes. On the advice of one of the lighthouse keepers on the islands, Archie sought out the man who pulled the strings and made it known that he was a loyal party member and wanted a job at one of the lighthouses. You see, the position of lighthouse keeper was, in Archie's era, one of very high social status. Most folks considered it to be on an equivalent social level with that of ships captain–thus even a job as a third assistant keeper would be a tremendous social step upward for Archie. It would, he thought, place him in a good position to gain Margie's notice at last. In late autumn the word came down that

ARCHIE'S STEPS

Archie was to meet with the keeper of the Raspberry Island lighthouse to see if the lad was of acceptable timber to work at the light.

It was during this same time that a man who some knew only as "Cooper" arrived in Bayfield and took a room in a local boarding house. He was a frightening sort of man with deep set eyes and a face that never had a smile. Shaking hands with him was much like holding a snake. Cooper made no secret of the fact that he had fought in the Civil War and had killed many a rebel with his lead shot and his bayonet, with the bayonet giving him the greatest satisfaction. He would often remark that he was sorry that the war was over because although the food was terrible, he truly missed "the work."

Exactly why Cooper was in the town of Bayfield was never known. Some said he had come to speculate on the infant timber industry while others said he was there for other, darker reasons–such as running from the law. Still, Cooper often could be found at events where the upper class of folks gathered. It was at just such a social party that Cooper met Margie. She was captivated by his dark background and razor edged manner. Over time the two of them became an item around town and Margie spent hours listening to his gory tales of death and killing. In fact, the more he detailed the last moments of human life the more Margie was thrilled. They developed a sick, yet intense bond that was cemented by images of war and killing.

Archie had easily gained the approval of the lighthouse keeper of Raspberry Island and was scheduled to take the position of second assistant keeper in the spring. As soon as he had the news in hand he sought out Margie so as to inform her of his impending new social status. It happened that Margie was in the company of Cooper when the newly selected lighthouse keeper came bounding up in his puppy dog manner. She attempted to simply brush him off, but he persisted. Cooper stepped in and a fairly nasty scene transpired. For most young men it would have been clear enough that this female had nothing but disdain for him, but Archie kept pestering Margie as if she had failed to understand his accomplishment. Often Cooper was there to deflect Archie and more often Margie was purely impolite. Archie told her that once he was hauling oil up to that light and responsible for safely guiding countless vessels across the lake, she would change her tune. This pathetic drama continued into the winter months, with Archie boasting of how he had made something of himself and Margie treating him as a repulsive sore upon her life.

Finally in mid-December the keeper of the lighthouse asked Archie to tend to the property while the keeper and his family went to Superior for the holiday. The lighthouse had been deactivated for the season, but the keeper was not yet ready to shut the place up for the winter. Archie would simply act as a care-taker until early January. This was a task that Archie happily accepted and soon found himself in charge of the Raspberry Island lighthouse. Many a night he spent climbing up into the tower and looking at the winter sky. He often imagined that his Margie would have a change of heart and make the sleigh ride across the ice and out to his lighthouse. There she would be so impressed that she would see him in a far different light. Unfortunately for Archie, his focus of affection had no heart.

What actually happened to Archie remains a mystery. All that is known is that he vanished from Raspberry Island that winter. When the lighthouse keeper returned to seal up the station in January he found everything to be in order, except for the fact that there was no heat and everything was frozen. Archie was simply missing. Later the keeper went to Bayfield to find the young man and give him a good lecture about abandoning his responsibility, but no one had seen Archie in nearly a month. There were plenty of rumors that followed and most of them surrounded the fact that two significant people had suddenly packed up and left town for places unknown. Both Cooper and Margie had run off together and in a small town such as Bayfield it was easy to formulate an unspeakable formula that solved the mystery of Archie, Margie and Cooper.

Spoken in hushed terms, the speculation of what became of Archie involved Margie actually making that sleigh ride out to Raspberry Island. The intent that led the team of horses across the ice that night was not one of affection, but rather one of a sadistic thrill. Margie wanted to experience first hand what it was like to see a human life snuffed out and her instrument of fulfillment would be Cooper—her intended victim was Archie. We can only imagine the elation when Archie saw Margie at the door and his horror when Cooper appeared and the two of them dragged him off and butchered him just for the thrill of it.

Anna and Mary listened intently to the story while hiding under a table. They did not fully understand most of the implications, but most of the story sunk in. For the rest of the time they were at the lighthouse, they played and had fun, but they kept a close ear tuned for the sound of Archie's footsteps. Unfortunately, the steps were not heard again by the girls before they traveled back to the farm. For the rest of their lives the two little girls remembered the sound of those heavy, sad boots upon those wooden steps.

Years passed and eventually the Coast Guard automated the light on Raspberry Island. The lamp within the lighthouse tower was replaced by a lamp on a post that was placed in front of the building in 1957. Traffic through the west channel began to decline in the 1980s and eventually all of the lighthouses in the Apostle Island chain were handed over to the National Park service for preservation. The city of Bayfield still retains many of its lumber baron homes, but has transformed itself from a fishing village to a sparkling tourist town. The value of the islands and lighthouses is exploited by way of a small fleet of modern tour boats that regularly take tourists out to the islands where they can disembark and walk the grounds. At Raspberry Island tourists are met by park service guides and escorted up into the tower where they can see the view that Archie once pondered. When asked, the park rangers say that they are vaguely familiar with the story of Archie, but admit that in all of their time at the lighthouse they have never heard the steps. Still others in the area have all sorts of versions of the same story to tell. The exact story is known only to Archie.

REINDEER

No sooner had Captain Dunn eased the bow of the schooner *Reindeer* up to the wharf than all three men who had been his crew leaped ashore and headed "up the street" as fast as they could.

"Go on ya' superstitious cowards," the ship's master growled toward the departing crew, "Run like the bunch of rats that ya' are. I'm happy to be rid of the whole lot of ya!"

Of course nothing could be farther from the truth. He needed hands to operate the boat and now he would have to muster a new crew. Lucky was he that the crew had decided to jump ship in the sailor's town of Toronto. It was the mid 1800s and there were plenty of mariners for hire in this city. It was simply a matter of hitting the right tavern as well as making sure that the saloon he selected had also not been visited by any of his former crew. Once their tale of what had been happening aboard the *Reindeer* began to get around the waterfront, the mariners wanting to ship out on her would get very scarce. As the good captain made his way he came upon sleeping drunks and beleaguered tramps. Every now and then there was a mumbling lunatic. None of these men would be Captain Dunn's first choice as crew material, but after what had just happened aboard his boat a benumbed drunk just may be what he needed. Still, there were plenty of sober sailors looking for a berth and some of those may stay on for a trip or two. After a short bit of tramping around the piers the crusty old schooner captain had rounded up another crew of three and one of them was actually a cook. By the following afternoon they had the *Reindeer* loaded and once again headed out onto Lake Ontario.

Among the three men who had been recruited by Captain Dunn to man his vessel, Ben was the youngest. He was an energetic Canadian who had made his way down from the Georgian Bay area seeking a life of adventure as a mariner. So far all that he had found was plenty of work and too many bad meals. As he made himself at home aboard the *Reindeer* he had no idea that adventure of a different kind was stalking him.

It was a fine late summer day and fair winds soon filled the boat's sails. She was bound for Oswego and as darkness settled over the boat and her crew, Captain Dunn was in hope that the night would be a peaceful one. By one o'clock in the morning that fine breeze had gone and the *Reindeer* was left in nearly mid-lake, becalmed. There was nothing to navigate and so the tired master decided to crawl into his bunk and draw his curtain. Likewise, two of the other crew retired and left a single man on watch. The night was so calm that the schooner's sails hung like limp rags and the boat itself squatted on the lake's surface and hardly gave a twitch. The air was clear and muggy with heavy summer hanging about and there was no moon to split the blackness. In the cabin, the air seemed so thick that you could slice it. As a result, Ben decided to sleep out on deck. Grabbing a makeshift pillow that he had created from a sack that was stuffed with his extra clothing, the sleepy and overheated crewman headed for the boat's bow intending to curl up near the windlass. As he slowly made his way, he passed the crewman on watch, Ben said he was heading forward because it was too stuffy down there. With his clay pipe clenched tightly in his teeth the watchman simply grunted approval. Moments later the deck was again silent as the night went on.

All of the men selected by Captain Dunn were strangers to one another and none of them gave a hoot about the other. They were simply looking for a day's pay from sailing. It was a common practice in this era for sailors to ship out as total strangers and then sail a trip or two and part company. Often they hardly knew each others names. Ben didn't know the watchman's name and likewise, the watchman had no interest in Ben or where he decided to make his bed that night.

As the watchman sat quietly pondering the night something overhead caught his attention. At first he thought it to be some birds, then perhaps some sort of cloud. As he tried to focus, the misty vision swooped gracefully around the masts and up and around the sails. Clouds can move around like that he reasoned as the strange vision stopped and hovered. For a long moment he tried to focus on just what it may be and then his brain figured out the shape. It was a woman, hovering there among the mast tops. His mouth dropped slowly open and his pipe fell to the deck. His sense of wonder was soon turned to fright as the apparition simply floated high over the boat. All that he could think of was to wake the guy sleeping at the bow and show him the specter. Stumbling forward he nearly tripped over the sleeping Ben.

"Wake up!" He shook the snoozing sailor, "Wake up, you gotta' see this !"

"See what, see what?!" In a daze, Ben was shocked into consciousness.

"Up there in the riggin', sure if there ain't a ghost floatin'!"

"Up where?…what?" a dazed Ben did his best to clear his eyes and look where the watchman was pointing. "There ain't nothin' up there ya coot!" he objected, "You've gone loony!"

As the watchman looked up he saw that indeed there was nothing to be seen. Ben returned to his slumber, but the watchman did not have to worry about falling asleep himself–he was too spooked. As he walked the decks that night he kept getting the feeling that someone was behind him, he got to the point where he was afraid to turn around. Even though it was a warm night, the hair on the back of his neck tingled. Finally it got to the point where he simply sat with his back to the cabin and his eyes turned upward, waiting for the lady's return.

Just before dawn, Captain Dunn awoke to feel his boat sailing beneath his feet with a fair wind in her canvas. As he stepped through the companionway he found the wheel lashed and no one at the helm. A quick look around told him that indeed there was no one steering the ship, she was simply gliding away upon the wide open lake! He took a few moments to assure that the *Reindeer* was on her proper heading and then he set out to find out what had happened to his watchman. As he rounded the deckhouse, his answer was clear. There, propped up against the deckhouse, whisky bottle in hand was his night watchman–stone cold drunk and passed out. A stream of curse words came bellowing from the enraged captain as he relieved the intoxicated sailor of the brown bottle with a swift kick. The bottle went flipping into Lake Ontario and the watchman began to flail around in a confused panic. The commotion brought the rest of the crew to the scene just in time to witness the captain attempting to slap the drunken sailor back to sobriety. Ben and his fellow sober sailor, the cook, stepped in to stop the beating.

"Take that drunken dog and lock him in the fo'c'sle!" the captain roared, "I won't have the likes of him stinkin' up a bunk!"

The two remaining crewmen took hold of the intoxicated watchman and dragged him forward. With a measure of civility they placed him in the fo'c'sle. The cook simply wiped his hands of the problem and left while Ben remained and tried to help the drunk return to his senses.

Captain Dunn took his boat's wheel himself and now tried to assure himself that the vessel was headed in the proper direction. He had no idea how long the boat

had been sailing on her own and so also had no idea
if they were still on course for Oswego. As he steered
her on an east, southeast heading he was still stewing
about having taken a drunk aboard as a crewman. In
short order Ben came up, hands on hips and reported
the safe stowing of the drunken watchman.

"He's put away." Ben quipped.

Captain Dunn snarled a confirmation.

"He must have had the bottle hid in his bag," Ben
went on, "must have gone and got it while everyone
was asleep. He keeps jabberin' on about some woman
flyin' in the mastheads last night. I think he's been too
deep in that bottle too long, he's seein' things."

This time the captain did not reply, in fact his scowl
turned more toward a look of dread.

Sunset found the *Reindeer* still making her way
across the open lake with the wind rapidly fading from
her sails. Captain Dunn had his dinner down in the
cabin while the cook and Ben took the time to eat up
on the deck. In the fo'c'sle, the banished watchman
had regained most of his senses and was eating his
dinner in solitude. His encounter with the ghostly lady
who drifted about in the vessel's rigging had driven
him to his hidden bottle and now he was in no mood
to go out on deck, especially if it meant standing
another night watch. Captain Dunn's orders that he
remain confined in the musty fo'c'sle were just fine
with him. There was no desire on his part to see the
floating lady again.

Up on deck as the blackness of the night grew deep,
the stars came out and sparkled across the sky like a
handful of glitter tossed into the air. There was none of

the previous evening's haze and lights could be seen in the far distance. The only trouble for Captain Dunn was that once again the wind had died and the *Reindeer* was becalmed once more. Whether it was that Captain Dunn did not want a repeat of the previous night's incident or it was that he knew what this night would bring, the good captain decided to stand the night's watch himself. In the wee hours of that star-filled night Ben came out on deck for some fresh air. He tried to hold a brief conversation with the captain, but the dialogue was highly one sided as Captain Dunn only grunted responses. Feeling a bit awkward Ben tried to look casual as he stretched his legs and walked along the deck looking up at the stars. It was then that the screams of terror began.

From the fo'c'sle, the sound was as if a tiger had gotten in with that poor watchman. The thuds of his body bouncing off of the walls and his fists pounding upon the door echoed across Lake Ontario. No sooner had the captain and Ben headed forward than the watchman broke the latch and burst through the door and onto the deck.

"She's in there!" he screamed as he rolled across the deck like he had been set afire. "She's in there I tell you! She's in there!"

"Yer' just seein' things!" Ben stated convincingly as he grabbed the watchman by the shoulders. "It's that demon rum has got to ya!"

"No, no…" the watchman sobbed as he lay sprawled on the deck with his legs pumping as it to kick his way from the fo'c'sle door. "She was in there, she looked right at me!" Looking up toward Ben the watchman suddenly went silent as his mouth opened wide and his eyes focused straight up. "There she is again!" he screamed, pointing toward the mast tops.

Instinctively the captain and Ben both looked up and there, hovering in the high rigging, was the translucent white specter of a woman. Silently drifting around as if pushed by a breeze from beyond. For a long moment all three men simply gazed at her and then three very different reactions were produced. The terrified watchman began to scream and cry like a little child awakening in a nightmare. Ben, who had been holding the watchman, dropped his fellow mariner and gasped a curse word of astonishment. Captain Dunn's reaction, however, was quite out of place.

"You witch!" he bellowed as he shook his fist toward the apparition. "Why can't ya' leave me alone, why can't ya' leave me be!"

The ghost simply hovered in the mast tops like a cloud. Then she moved playfully among the sails and suddenly vanished.

For a long moment Ben sat stunned. Then he began to zigzag around the deck searching skyward for another sighting of the hovering spirit, but she was gone. Captain Dunn growled and stomped back toward the wheel while the watchman crumbled to the deck in a sobbing heap. When it became clear that the ghost was gone, Ben came to the helm and bubbling with curiosity, he began to interrogate Captain Dunn.

"You've seen her before, haven't ya?"

"Mind yer' own business!" Dunn snapped.

"Ya' talked like you've seen her before." Ben circled the captain, "That's why you needed a new crew in Toronto. This boat's haunted ain't it?"

"I said ya' mind yer' business and quit yappin' at me," Dunn scowled in a low voice, "or you'll be locked in the fo'c'sle along with that other drunk."

"How long has she been comin' here?" Ben persisted.

Captain Dunn stood silently gripping the wheel spokes as if his fingers were around Ben's throat.

"Your last crew found out this boat was haunted and figurin' it's got a hoodoo on it they jumped in port eh?"

Oddly, Ben seemed more inquisitive than frightened, but Captain Dunn didn't want any part of it. Finally he'd had enough of the crewman's questioning.

"You get away from me or I'll flatten yer' nose!" Dunn snarled.

Ben knew when he was at the end of the rope and he stopped asking questions and headed up toward the fo'c'sle to try and put the watchman back together again. Curled in a ball and whimpering like a baby, the watchman could only beg not to go back into the fo'c'sle. Ben assured him that he would not have to be locked up again and that they would both stay awake together until the sun came up. His statement did little to calm the watchman and through the remainder of the night he stayed in a state of shock.

Oswego's lighthouse could not have been a more welcome sight for the crew of the *Reindeer.* Much the same as had occurred in Toronto, the entire crew took their dunnage in hand and went over the side as soon as the boat's rail was close enough to make the jump. The boat's cook, who had slept through both of the hauntings was informed by his shipmates of the ghost's appearances and being a highly superstitious fellow, he jumped ship just on the word that the boat was haunted. As he went ashore the cook turned to Captain Dunn and gave a cryptic warning.

"There's a hoodoo on yer' boat," the superstitious cook shouted loud enough for the whole waterfront to hear, "and as sure as you can bet, that ghost is gonna come and take you with her!"

Ben simply huffed his sailor's bag over his shoulder and walked up the street. He kept looking back toward the *Reindeer* and Captain Dunn. The captain seemed resigned to simply start all over again and went into the deckhouse. For a time Ben felt a bit guilty about abandoning the poor soul and his boat. Still, a hoodoo was a hoodoo and so there was no way that Ben was sailing on that boat again.

As Ben and the cook came upon a local saloon, Ben invited his former shipmate in for some food and a drink. The cook refused, saying that Ben had seen the ghost with his own eyes and that made him bad luck too. The cook kept walking at a fast pace and told Ben that he should steer away from him if their paths ever crossed again.

Saloons in this era were a far cry from the depiction of such establishments in Hollywood wild west movies. The one that Ben happened into this day was a narrow room with a short bar and propensity for serving good food. Ben found himself a seat and began telling the saloon keeper of the ghost and the *Reindeer*. His tale caught the ear of a fellow sitting nearby and the man interrupted Ben's story.

"That ain't the first time." The man chimed in, "I got off her in Port Colborne last November because of that witch."

With Ben and the saloon keeper listening intently, the man told the tale of how the boat had been fighting a fierce gale when up in the mast tops there appeared the ghost of the vessel's former cook. Several years before she had been working on laundry in the fo'c'sle when the boat was in a collision with another vessel. She was crushed to death by the timbers as the two boats came together.

"I got on her in Port Colborne and we headed for Toronto." The man yarned, "No sooner do we get out on the open lake than this wind comes a boomin' with snow like you never saw. Got so bad that Dunn had to turn and run back for Port Colborne. It was then that we saw her floatin' in the rigging. None of us thought we'd see land again. Thought for sure she was gonna take us with her. We only found out when the boat got back to Port Colborne and started telling the story that old Dunn had renamed the boat a few times because he can't get crews."

"Well Oswego ain't Port Colborne," the saloon keeper quipped out of the corner of his mouth, "and it ain't Toronto neither. There ain't much room on these docks and the word gets around fast. Dunn won't be takin' none of our sailin' men out on his hoodoo boat."

"Oh he'll get him a crew all right," the man smirked as he slid back in his chair, "his kind always find a way."

Now Ben didn't feel quite so sorry for Captain Dunn. As the saloon conversation wore on he found that the man who had been telling the story was the mate on a sailing boat. It was a canaller and headed for the western lakes. Before he knew it, Ben had himself a new berth and a new job. Within a few hours he was

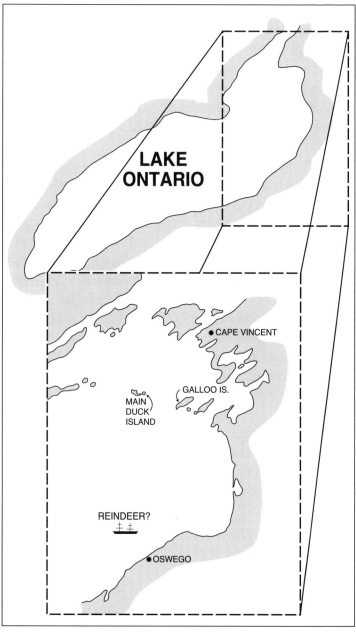

aboard and making ready for the trip. As he got involved in the ships work, Ben was suddenly grabbed by the shirt sleeve by the mate.

"Come here kid," the mate ordered, "wanna show ya' somethin'."

As the two men walked to the boats rail the mate pointed toward the harbor entrance.

"Look over there." he said knowingly.

There, on the end of a towing hawser connected to one of the local harbor tugs, was the *Reindeer,* on her way into the open lake.

"Like I told ya'..." the mate boasted, "Old Dunn got himself another crew. His kind always does."

Ben just shook his head. "He probably renamed her again just to get guys and take 'em all away with her."

Ben did not get back to Oswego for nearly a year. By then it was his second season on the boat and he had tall tales of upper lake gales to tell. He dropped into that saloon that he had been in after his trip on the *Reindeer* and again struck up a conversation with the owner. When Ben mentioned the *Reindeer*, the saloon keeper simply froze for a second. Then he leaned on the bar and informed Ben that when the *Reindeer* left port that day, it was the last time she was ever seen. The boat had vanished with all hands amid a calm summer night.

SPIRITS OF THE POINT

Normally, as an author, the writer of this text attempts to not repeat a given story in more than one book. However, in the case of the Pointe aux Barques lighthouse, and the story of the mysterious lady who inhabits the site, the following firsthand account is just too compelling to resist placing within these pages. Additionally, I have obtained some new information that may give us a clue as to her identity. It is one thing to tell you a ghost "story" but it is quite another thing when I can tell you the ghost's name.

In researching and creating the story of the Pointe aux Barques lighthouse ghost, the author found it necessary to travel to that location and obtain additional photographs of the keeper's quarters to illustrate the tale. The day was overcast with thin gray clouds and the view across the lake was limited by a thick haze on that unusually warm November day as I dashed around the property and snapped photos of the assorted buildings. All of the structures had been locked up tightly for the winter since early October and I was the only person on the grounds. As any

This photo was taken first. Notice the closed curtains in all windows–then I stepped 50 feet to my left and...

photographer would do, I snapped about two rolls of film and captured the buildings from assorted angles. In photographing the keeper's house where Pamela Kennedy had encountered the apparition that is featured in this chapter, I found a clear shot of the front that captured the whole house, then stepped about 50-feet to my left and shot again. About a week later, the film was sent out for processing and returned a day later as finished. Bringing the packages containing the photographs home I spread them out on the coffee table and gave each a quick inspection before returning them to their respective envelopes. Two weeks later, I was carefully sorting out the artwork that was to be used in this book and when I got to this chapter I took a good look at the photos of the keeper's house. Of the two best, one was of good contrast and background and could certainly be used, the other

SPIRITS OF THE POINT

*...took this one. Note that someone is peeking from the window. This is **not** a reflection. Author's Collection*

appeared to be a throwaway, because the nose of my car was in the background... it was while making that decision that I saw it. There in the upper front bedroom window, there appeared to be the image of someone pulling aside the sheer curtains and looking out of the window, but in the photo that was taken just 90 seconds earlier and from 50-feet to the left, those same curtains appear to be tightly closed!

Being a skeptic, a researcher and born cynic, I could not allow myself to believe my eyes. Certainly I had been predisposed to wanting to "see" something there in that window. Perhaps it was a reflection of a branch from some tree in front of the house, or perhaps a defect in the print. I looked at the other photos and saw that there are no trees of the size needed to make such a reflection located in front of that window. Moreover, any such reflection would continue on a line into the adjacent window–this image did not. Next I grabbed my camera and removed the 50 mm lens. Using it like a jeweler's loop I magnified the image for my eye–there was someone there, looking out toward the park area behind the lighthouse. There appeared to be a translucent face and the image appeared to be wearing a high collared white dress. Still convinced that I was talking myself into seeing things, I took the photo upstairs where my wife and sister-in-law were baking Christmas cookies. My sister-in-law Karen had absolutely no knowledge of any aspect of this story so, handing her the photo I asked simply, "Look at those windows and tell me what you see?"

Without an instants hesitation she said, "You mean that one there with someone lookin' out of it?"

Her comment knocked me three steps backward, and a wave of chilled shock came across me the likes of which I have never before experienced. I am a professional aviator, a trained observer with a college degree in the sciences, my training causes me to think in terms of physics, facts, limitations, rules and data, but I was holding in my hand a photo of a ghost, and there was no way for me to discount the photographer, because I had taken it myself. In the hours that followed I obtained the negative, and the specter in the window showed up there as well. I scanned the photo into my computer, and enlarged it, enhanced it, reversed it, adjusted it–still the image in the window was there and without explanation. I knew now how Pamela Kennedy must have felt after her encounter with the strange lady that haunts the Pointe aux

Barques lighthouse. With that in mind I quickly called Pamela. I asked her to recall everyone who had scoffed at her sighting of the ghost and then told her to call them up and set them straight. They all needed to be told that Pamela Kennedy was not seeing things, because I had the proof, I had the Pointe aux Barques lighthouse ghost on film!

When the United States Coast Guard elected to turn the property containing the lighthouse over to the private sector in 1958, the local county was farsighted enough to jump on the opportunity and take charge of the site. Since that point, the light itself has been in the hands of the Coast Guard, but everything surrounding the tower became county property. The original keeper's residence attached to the tower was converted into a maritime museum, and the grounds made into a camping area. To maintain the site, the county has taken to hiring a series of grounds keepers to reside in the newer keeper's dwelling and watch over the facility in general. Enter Ray and Martha Janderwski, in 1992 they became the grounds keepers. For both Ray and Martha, the job must have been a unique opportunity, after all they were actually being paid to reside in one of the most beautiful locations on the Great Lakes and to look after one of the most beautiful lighthouses on the lakes as well. What neither of them could know was that there was already a lady watching over the lighthouse and hers was a vigil that would never, ever, end.

A light was established on Pointe aux Barques in 1847, but the current standing tower was not constructed until 1857. It was originally listed as having a fixed white light with a third order optic that was visible for 7 miles. Later listings, however show the light as being a flashing white light that osculated at 10 second intervals and was visible for 16 and one half miles. Listings between 1857 and 1880 also vary in the height of the light with the 1857 listing showing it as being 65-feet tall and the 1880 listing showing it as being 79-feet tall. This is easily explained by the fact that the 1857 records used the height from the base of the tower to the center of the beacon. The 1880 listing, on the other hand, used "focal plain" which is the distance from the average water level to the center of the beacon. Since the lighthouse is constructed upon

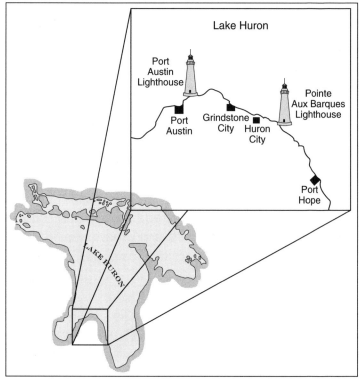

a small bluff, the difference in the two listings is the height of the bluff above Lake Huron. The difference in the distance from which the light can be viewed is likely due to an 1873 refit of the lamp. It is probable that the new "flashing" characteristic was installed at that time as well.

Soon after Martha and Ray took charge of the lighthouse grounds, they began asking their adult daughter, Pamela to come and spend the night in the historic keeper's quarters that was now in their charge. Pamela had been to the lighthouse a number of times, but really had no desire to stay there. For some reason that she could not explain, the place just gave her the creeps, in fact, she plain did not like being there. Now, Pamela is just as average a person as you would ever want to meet in mid-Michigan. She had never had any type of excursion into the supernatural other than reading her horoscope in the newspaper and then watching the predictions not come true. Still, there was something about that lighthouse and particularly that keeper's residence that gave her a bad feeling that she could not explain.

As it is with all children who have grown to become adults, the pressure to satisfy ones parents can grow far larger than any unexplained bad feelings such as those that Pamela felt about the lighthouse. So it was that one day during the first summer that Ray and Martha were tending the property, Pamela simply gave in and agreed to spend the night at Pointe aux Barques with her folks. After all, what could happen? She was to be residing so far from any of the woes of the big cities that any evil-doers of the metropolitan areas would likely get lost before finding her. The most fearful noise that would occur would be the gentle lapping of Lake Huron's waves upon the nearby beach and about the only excitement that one may expect would be if one of the local cows got loose. Certainly, that bad feeling that she had was simply nonsense. Besides, there was also "Shadow" the family dog keeping a watch on her and the house. She would be as safe as she could ever imagine. At least, that is what she kept telling herself as she settled into the upstairs west bedroom. Indeed she was absolutely correct in that assumption, because she was being watched over constantly, but during that night, Shadow the dog had help watching over Pamela.

After some fitful tossing and turning, Pamela finally slipped into a state of quiet slumber. Late into the night, for reasons that she could not fathom, Pamela suddenly awakened. It was the kind of unexplained, middle of the night awakening that we have all experienced, where your eyes suddenly pop open and you lay there completely alert for no reason whatsoever. The room was quiet and the house was peaceful, and there was no apparent commotion, yet something had drawn Pamela from her sleep. Looking around she noticed that Shadow, the lovable mutt was laying just outside her door intently gazing down the stairway. Pamela muttered the series of rhetorical verbal commands that most people would speak toward a silly pet doing something strange. The dog ignored her and remained fixated on the stairway. Finally, Pamela decided that she would find out what was the matter with the family dog, and got out of bed.

Although closed for the season, the light at Pointe aux Barques stands tall against Lake Huron. Note the date "1857" above the walkway door. Author's Collection

Making her way toward the door she noticed that Shadow the dog, unusually, did not look toward her as she approached, but continued to gaze down the stairs. As she approached the dog and again asked what was the matter, Pamela glanced in the direction in which Shadow was peering. To her shock, she saw that there was a woman standing at the bottom of the stairs.

Garbed in a long cottony dress, the lady at the bottom of the stairway appeared to be aged about in her mid 30s and was very slim. Her dress was long sleeved, of a light color, had a printed pattern and a high collar. Around her waist was tied a long kitchen apron whose upper portion had been folded down, as if she were in the middle of cooking or cleaning. The lady wore her hair tied back in a very old fashioned manner and simply stood at the bottom of the steps with one hand placed upon the banister all the while looking directly up at Pamela.

It was an event that most of us would consider terrifying. Yet, standing in a darkened old house in the middle of the night looking directly into the face of a ghost, Pamela Kennedy was neither terrified nor shocked. Oddly, she felt greatly at ease, as if being welcomed in some way. For a long moment the two stood and gazed at one another and Pamela almost expected the spectral lady to speak. Suddenly, the female apparition simply turned and walked away through the door and toward the lighthouse. A sense of pure relief cascaded over Pamela, and she returned to bed feeling as if she now was welcome at both the lighthouse and the keeper's quarters.

At breakfast the following morning, Pamela sat down with Martha and Ray and the family engaged in the normal early morning small-talk. Somewhere within the conversation Pamela casually mentioned that her parents should not worry about the lady in the house

SPIRITS OF THE POINT

with them, because she was not there to hurt anyone, she was simply hanging out. The room went silent as her parents froze with shock.

"What lady?" they both asked.

"The lady, you know..." Pamela responded in a matter of fact tone, "the ghost, the ghost that lives at the lighthouse."

Neither Martha nor Ray had ever had a hint of any ghost residing on the property.

So, just who is this spectral lady of the lakes? There are several possibilities, but first we must look closely at Pamela's description of the lady. Although, upon personal interview, it was found that Pamela had scant knowledge of the garb and appearance of ladies of pre-depression era, and little knowledge about the fact that ladies worked the lakes aboard vessels long ago, her description has some interesting details. Although when talking about a ghost sighting, you are always dealing with pure hearsay and speculation we can draw some interesting conclusions. First, it is commonly held among those who deal with apparitions and their appearances, that the ghosts often appear dressed in clothing that they were the most often clad in, and thus most comfortable being seen in. Also, it is common for apparitions to be dressed in the clothing that they were wearing at the time of their death. Additionally, it is thought that the ghost of a person will remain at a given location because of some sort of connection to that location in life or at the time of death. The dress worn by the individual sounds very much as if it befits a woman of the 1850s to 1900s era. Additionally, the light colored fabric would indicate summer garb. The apron worn tied around the waist with the upper portion folded down indicates someone who performs household type work, but not currently engaged in such work.

In looking closely at the records of the events that took place at Pointe aux Barques, there is only one consistent official source and that is the Annual Reports of the United States Life Saving Service which, in 1876, established a station just 500-feet away from the lighthouse keeper's quarters where Pamela saw her ghost. In the hope that tragic events occurring at the lighthouse may be reflected in these reports, the volumes from 1876 to 1913 were completely searched, but yielded nothing. The complete holdings of the National Archives concerning the Pointe aux Barques lighthouse were searched and, sparse as these holdings are, they also yielded no clues. According to the National Archives, no logbooks from the Pointe aux Barques lighthouse are known to exist. Speculation may also lead us to the possibility that this lady of the light is someone lost in a nearby shipwreck. There are more than 30 shipwrecks which may have involved the loss of life that are known to have taken place in the general vicinity of the lighthouse, 14 of which are documented as fatal. Some of these shipwrecks may have involved female cooks among their victims, but a complete research of all of these wrecks is not yet finished. We do know, that in at least two cases, ladies of the lakes who fit the description of the Pointe aux Barques lighthouse ghost are documented to having been lost in the area.

On August 20th, 1899, the schooner *Hunter Savidge* was capsized by a summer squall and five of

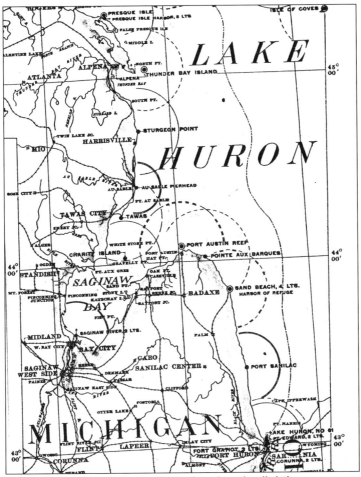

General map from 1892 showing the lighthouses of Michigan's thumb.

her crew were lost. This fatality included the captain's wife, Rosa Sharpsteen along with the vessel owner's wife, Mary Muellerweiss and her six year old daughter. Accounts indicate that Rosa was far to old to fit the description of the ghost, but Mary does fit the profile.

Additionally, the *Hunter Savidge* was lost on a repressively hot summer day, and the lost lady would have been garbed in light colored summer clothing as described by Pamela. On the 23rd day of May, 1910, the 436-foot oreboat *Frank H. Goodyear* collided with the oreboat *James B. Wood* in the general area of Pointe aux Barques. The *Goodyear* went to Lake Huron's bottom in minutes and just as quickly left her people in the water, struggling for survival. Among those who managed to surface after the sinking was Lillian Bassett, the wife of the ship's cook. She had been in the galley helping her spouse clean up after breakfast when the collision occurred. Moments after she surfaced, one of the *Goodyear's* massive and heavy wooden hatch-planks shot up end-wise from under the water and then slammed down upon her as she bobbed in the lake with her infant son in her arms. She too was likely wearing the garb described by Pamela and would likely fit the description of the lady who haunts the lighthouse. The complete story of the

The *Frank H. Goodyear, before it collided with the oreboat* James B. Wood. *Author's Collection*

SPIRITS OF THE POINT

Hull planking from an old wooden shipwreck, cast up onto the point by a recent storm, is stored behind the lighthouse. Author's Collection

Goodyear wreck can be found in this author's book, "Stormy Disasters". Oddly, both Mary and Lillian were lost with children in arms. Next, there is a lady listed as having been washed overboard from a vessel in November of 1901. This event is still being researched, and may or may not lend some insight to this story.

There is also the cynic's reasoning that Pamela may just be making the whole thing up, or may have simply dreamed the whole event. This conclusion can be discounted for two reasons. First, being a person who upon interview demonstrated limited knowledge of the garb and manner of the ladies of the old lakes, her description of the specter seems too accurate to have come from anyone but a historian or eyewitness. Second, there are plenty of ghost stories to go around on Pointe aux Barques, and it is an area that even the most hardened research historian, such as this author, has to admit is haunted.

Following my original publication of this story the image of that ghost in the window haunted me as much as the ghost itself haunts the lighthouse. As a good research historian, I found it impossible to stop digging into the story and while doing a book signing in nearby Harbor Beach, I happened to strike up a conversation with some members of the local genealogical society. They pointed me toward some local material that named the first keepers of the Pointe aux Barques lighthouse. In 1847 the survey was made for the construction of the very first lighthouse at that location. The lighthouse tower and keeper's quarters were constructed by gathering some of the large rocks that line the shore nearby. These local rocks were used like masonry and were mortared together to form the first Pointe aux Barques lighthouse whose lamp was lit in 1848. Prior to activation of the light, a keeper had to be assigned to the facility. A local pioneer, Peter Shook, took the assignment and both he and his wife Catherine moved out into the wilderness that was then Pointe aux Barques. It is important to remember that in that era, Pointe aux Barques was an extremely isolated place. The closest civilization was in Fort Gratiot, today known as Port Huron, and the only means of transportation was by sailing vessel in the summer months and by dog sled in the deep winter. In the early spring months and late autumn months the distance between Pointe aux Barques and the rest of the civilized world was impassable because of the mud and melting ice. The lighthouse was surrounded by thick forest and the ground that was cleared was nearly unsuitable for farming as it was studded with huge boulders and most of the soil was either clay or sand. The surrounding woods were not very friendly either. In this era there were still bears running wild. Yet Peter and Catherine Shook were expected to tend to the lighthouse and live off the land, all as a single responsibility.

Peter Shook's time at the Pointe aux Barques lighthouse was very limited as it is recorded that he died in 1849. Exactly what happened to him we do not know. The only information states that he "drown." It is likely that he accidentally drown while fishing near the lighthouse. Although we can only imagine the sorrow and isolation felt by Catherine following the death of her husband, she stayed on and tended to the lighthouse. For the next year, Catherine Shook diligently watched over the lighthouse and saw to the duties as its keeper. She also grew the food, killed the game, netted the fish and protected the property. In 1851 Francis Sweet was assigned to the Pointe aux Barques lighthouse as keeper and it was then that Catherine Shook stopped watching over the lighthouse–or did she? Perhaps it is Catherine Shook whose spirit still walks the grounds of the Pointe aux Barques lighthouse.

Discovering exactly who the people are who haunt Pointe aux Barques is a difficult and perhaps impossible task. Everyone who has encountered one of these specters swears that what they have seen is absolutely real, and most have been chanced in some way by the encounter. A yachtsman was spared the damage to his vessel by a surfboat filled with life-savers, the likes of which have not been seen on the lakes for nearly half a century, and went away certain that someone watches over Pointe aux Barques. Dennis Hale is sure that his life was saved by a mysterious ghost that knew how to survive the clutches of the lake. Pamela Kennedy never feels uncomfortable visiting, or staying at the lighthouse anymore. She is sure that the lady of the light watches over the place and considers Pamela to be a welcome guest. In all, the spirits that haunt the point apparently do so with good intent and so it should not matter exactly who they are.

DON'S ROWBOAT

In the months that followed World War II the nation was in a sort of transitional vacuum between the boom of war production and the return to peacetime normalcy. Huge quantities of war machines were being returned to U.S. soil and placed in stockpiles and the men who used those machines were coming home in huge numbers as well. The gap between G.I. and job was rapidly growing as the nation teetered between prosperity and the return of the Great Depression. Among that crowd was a young G.I. by the name of Don. He had gone into the Army in the middle of the war and found himself overseas pushing a pencil in the rear area instead of shooting bullets on the front lines. He had spent most of the war fighting boredom in a dried up desert instead of fighting the enemy on the European front. Still, in perspective, the war was won as much by those who tracked and shipped faceless crates of supplies as it was by those who battled at the front.

In the endless days of fly swatting and sweating, Don and his fellow supply soldiers had plenty of time to talk and dream of what they would do when this war ended. Don, being from mid-Michigan escaped the desert heat by yearning of those days when he was a kid and his uncle would take him out on the big lake in a little rowboat and the two of them would go out so far from shore that the land would fade from sight and there would be nothing but sparkling fresh water as far as the eye could see. The two of them would then fish the day away and according to the G.I.'s rosy daydream, they would return with a boat full of perch that would be fried and eaten in happy dinners that only a homesick soldier can imagine. As the war stretched out and the dry desert sapped more and more morale from the soul of the soldiers, Don's lake got bluer and those fish tasted better. Then with the end of the war in Europe, Don's unit had high hopes of soon being home. Those hopes soon faded as their deployment protracted well beyond V.J. Day. Finally came the day when Don and his buddies were placed in the bed of a truck and headed up the dusty road for home. At some faceless port they boarded a dull gray transport ship and began the crowded trip across the Atlantic for home.

The days crossing the pond and headed for the states were spent playing marathon poker games and telling anyone who would listen the stories of, "what I'm gonna do when I get back." Every one of the G.I.s had their own tales, most involving home or girls or a favored watering hole. Don had the Great Lakes and his rowboat. With each telling, the lake got more beautiful, the rowboat got more friendly and the pile of Don's fish got larger. By the time he reached his home, that tale of lake and fish had become a near obsession. Unfortunately for Don, he arrived home just in time for the winter ice to lock the lakes up tightly and hide those tons of fish under a roof of that frozen fresh water. Don's dream would have to wait until spring.

Through that winter there were far more veterans than there were jobs, and Don spent most of the winter getting reacquainted with being home and looking for odd jobs. Finally he landed work at a local gas station and happily went about pumping gas, checking oil and telling his tale of rowboats and fishing on the lake to anyone who would listen. Then came the day when Don's dream began to come true. A customer who had stopped into the station to have a punctured tire repaired listened to Don tell his story and offered to sell the former G.I. a small outboard motor for five dollars. All Don had to do was to get it to run. Using a 55 gallon drum filled with water and a lot of spare time, Don managed to get the motor to run, or at least to do a reasonable imitation of running. From that moment on Don's days ended with dreams of powering his way out onto the lake using his little outboard motor and a rowboat he had yet to acquire.

The next piece of Don's dream fell into place when a friend at the local drug store's lunch counter told Don that he knew of a place up north that rented both cabins by the lake and rowboats for fishing. With the exact name and location of the cottages, Don now needed only to wait for the next chance to go up and make his dream come true. There came a day in May when Don had the weekend off and after borrowing his cousin's pickup truck and placing his outboard motor aboard, he headed to that magical place that the folks in Michigan simply call "up north."

Up along the road between Alpena and Mackinaw City Don watched carefully for the sign that marked the cottages that he had been directed to. Suddenly, there it was, a row of tiny one-room cabins on the wrong side of the road and looking about as glamorous as an outhouse. As Don wheeled the pickup into the small parking lot, the dust formed a small cloud that alerted the owner's dog. Don shuffled toward the office and met with the owner who said that indeed he did have an available cabin and a boat for fishing. Don could hardly contain his excitement as he was led back to the small flat-bottom wooden rowboat. The owner of the cottages told him that the boat had held water last summer, but he was not going to guarantee that she would hold water this season. Don did not care, he simply asked for help putting the boat into his truck and wanted to know where he could put her in the water.

"Yer' not thinkin' of goin' out there now are ya'?" the cottage owner exclaimed.

"Well… yeah." Don replied.

"Naw," the cottage owner scoffed, "the winds blowin' and there's eight foot whitecaps, you won't make it fifty feet!"

Don looked across the street toward Lake Huron and his heart sank. The lake appeared to be raging with a chop that stretched to the horizon.

"Wait until morning," the cottage owner advised, "it'll be nice and smooth then and you can launch right down at the end of the road there."

DON'S ROWBOAT

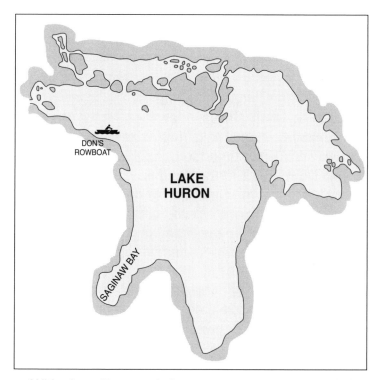

DON'S
ROWBOAT

LAKE
HURON

SAGINAW BAY

With that, Don and the cottage owner loaded the little rowboat into the truck bed and Don retired to his little cottage to wait for morning. The place smelled like no one had been in there in a decade and even with the windows open the musty atmosphere persisted. That evening Don went down and walked the beach before dark. Even with its chop, Lake Huron was as beautiful as it had been in his G.I. fantasies. It sparkled and almost called to him and Don felt like a boy once again. That night the sound of the waves rocked him to sleep and then the boom of thunder startled him back into consciousness. The flashing lightening grew more intense and the thunder grew louder as a vicious thunderstorm swept from inland toward the shore. Soon a swirl of screaming wind lashed at Don's little cottage and at times it felt as if the storm was bound to lift the closet size structure from the ground and toss it into the lake. Then came the rain hissing at the windows and walls. In just a few minutes the wind and rain died into a steady calm rhythm as the spring storm passed and Don returned to sleep.

Don did not wait for a breakfast invitation from the cabin's owner as he burst from his cottage at the crack of dawn. The air was thick and cool as a heavy fog that had been left over by the previous night's storm hung over the shore. The door slammed with a hollow metal echo as Don plopped into his pickup truck and started her up. Tooling the vehicle to the sandy road that led to Lake Huron, he discovered that the lake's mood had shifted for the better. Now the water was as smooth as a sheet of fine glass and Don wasted no time dragging the rowboat from the truck bed and shoving it into the water. There was no need to tie her up while he moved the truck to the side of the road, the lake was so calm that the little rowboat simply floated in place as if waiting to make Don's dream come true. Snatching a borrowed tackle box and fishing pole from the parked vehicle, Don marched happily toward the lake. The damp sand seemed to welcome each step as he walked to the water's edge and climbed aboard the boat. Clunking his gear aboard Don shoved off, settling onto the wooden seat. Several tugs on the outboard motor's starting rope caused the little engine to come to life in a cloud of blue oil smoke. Shortly thereafter Don was on his way onto the lake... for about 20 yards. There the motor simply died and refused to restart. Undeterred, Don decided to take to the oars and row. It was then that he realized that he had actually never rowed a boat before. Fumbling with the oars he managed to keep the little craft headed out into Lake Huron–it was a strange course, but still it would take him onto the open lake.

After about 45 minutes of rowing Don took the time to stop and look around. The fog was growing more dense and a wind was coming up that seemed to blow him away from shore. The shoreline itself had been swallowed by the mist and all Don could see was water. In fact, so thick had the fog become that he could only see a few yards from his boat in any direction. That was just fine with Don as he busied himself baiting his hook and before long was drowning a worm in Lake Huron's depths. Except for the fog, it was all exactly as he had pictured it, quiet, cool and relaxing. An occasional nibble on his line drew Don's attention as he drifted, both in mind and in person.

Exactly how much time passed was unclear. Don had left his watch in the cottage and so as the morning dragged on he had little concept of the hour. His attention, however, was drawn to that breeze that had been quietly blowing from off-shore. It had now turned into something of a wind and he could tell by the stretch of his fishing line that he was being blown along the lake's surface at a respectable pace. Having no idea how far from land he was, Don suddenly concluded that being blown by the wind was probably not the best condition to be in. At best, he would have extra rowing to get back to shore and at worst he could end up in

Canada in a few days. It struck him that he actually did not even know which way land was! The fog had swallowed him whole. Looking around the little rowboat he also realized that there was nothing at all aboard that could act as any sort of anchor. Suddenly his dream was becoming a nightmare. He was stuck there, drifting toward panic. He decided to get that motor going and began to fumble with the device. He decided that he would need to pull the outboard from its mount and perhaps perform some manly magic on its workings. Of course, the combination of rolling boat and bulky outboard motor quickly out balanced him and the greasy motor slipped from his grip and splashed into the lake. Don watched in horror as the motor rapidly vanished into the deep dark waters of Lake Huron, leaving behind an oily sheen of gas and oil.

It was then that the fog toward his right began to grow intensely dark. In fact, it began to turn into a huge dark wall as the bow of a giant lake freighter suddenly loomed from the mist. The mighty lakeboat was so close that Don found himself looking nearly straight up just to see her rail. When it became clear that he was not going to be run down by the boat, Don's thoughts went from panic to salvation. Surely someone aboard the big boat was on lookout and would hear him if he shouted. He would be saved from his foggy peril.

"Hey!" Don bellowed, "Ahoy there!" he shouted trying to sound nautical.

There was no response as the boats massive hull slid silently past. Don continued his shouts, but there was no one to be seen and no one that replied. There was not even a light on her deck. Soon the boat's stern

DON'S ROWBOAT

Painting by Susan Robinson.

approached and Don's shouts turned nearly to screams. He went from "Ahoy" to "Help!" but still there was no response–the big oreboat simply sailed past ignoring the little rowboat and its horrified passenger completely. Now Don's fear turned to anger as he saw that they were simply going to leave him behind as if he were an insignificant piece of driftwood. A chorus of shouted cuss words followed the big freighter as it vanished back into the fog. Don had just one act of revenge that he could inflict upon a vessel that would ignore a man in distress–he read her name and burned it into his brain.

For the better part of two hours Don sat and stewed in his little rowboat. Then the fog began to lift as overhead he saw the sun burn its way through the clouds. As the fog cleared, Don saw that he was only a few miles from shore. Lakefront cottages and trees were clearly visible and he turned the boat and made haste in rowing back to land. Try as he may, he could not spot the place on the shoreline where he had parked the truck and launched the boat, so he simply pointed himself toward land and pulled at the oars. Happily he heard the sound of the beach as it came grinding under the rowboat. He dropped the oars and jumped onto the beach in relief. It was then that he noticed he had never taken his fishing line from the water. Retrieving the pole Don reeled the line in. At its end was only a hook and parts of a badly drown worm. After walking up and down the beach he managed to find his truck and then rowed the boat back to its launch site. He had missed coming ashore at the right spot by just a half mile, and had hiked in the wrong direction seeking his truck. When he went back the other way he found it in just a few minutes. Once the boat was returned to its owner, Don paid his bill and departed leaving the cottage owner with a venomous version of his tale. By midnight he was back home and his dream of going out on the lake was safely put away forever.

Decades passed and Don went about living his life, and its events far overshadowed that day on the lake. Still, he never really forgot that boat that left him behind without so much as a whistle toot. It was only the boredom of retirement and the nagging of his wife that caused him to visit a maritime festival some 50 years after that foggy day on Lake Huron. While strolling about the festival, Don happened upon a Great Lakes historian who was holding court at a book signing table. Don had long been curious as to what had ever become of that damned freighter that had abandoned him. He struck up a conversation with the historian and told him the tale.

DON'S ROWBOAT

"Do you recall the name of the boat?" Don was asked.

"Oh I'll never forget that," Don groaned shaking his head. "It was *Curnthers.*"

"There's never been any such boat that I know of." The historian pondered.

James Curnthers," Don insisted, "I remember like it was yesterday."

When asked if the name may have been *James Carruthers*, Don's eyes widened.

"Yeah! That was it!" he exclaimed in satisfied recall.

Shuffling through several books on a nearby sales shelf, the historian produced one that had a series of vessel photos in it. Turning to a page with several pictures on it, the historian covered the photo captions with his fingers and asked Don if his boat was among those pictured. Without hesitation Don selected the image of the *James Carruthers*.

After being told that the boat he had shouted to in the late 1940s had been lost with all hands on Lake Huron in 1913 and was still missing, Don's expression turned to confusion. Several moments of confusion and rehashing the name followed. Then Don raised his eyebrows above his bifocal glasses and gave a matter-of-fact "humph."

"No wonder they didn't answer me." He said.

BEACHCOMBING FOR ETERNITY

Tickles the dog got her name by being the most affectionate and energetic animal to ever walk on four legs. A mutt with some Labradorean extraction, she got her name as a puppy and it was related to her habit of bounding upon small children and licking their faces until they began to giggle as if being tickled by a giant stuffed animal toy. Tina, Tickles' owner, had the hope that the dog would outgrow this habit. Tina, however, was wrong and Tickles remained an overly playful dog as she became an adult.

Indian summer had made an appearance on the Canadian coast of Lake Ontario and turned a normally dark November weekend into a simple pleasant autumn. Tina had been visiting friends who lived in the wonderful little town of Consecon, Ontario and she had found that Tickles loved the trip to the lakefront which was only a short drive away. Consecon itself was a refreshing break from Toronto's bustle and Tina's apartment in the city. It had taken a bit of exploring, but she and Tickles had managed to find a stretch of beach that was abandoned by the summer campers and seasonal residents. This secret spot was just right for walking the dog and bit of beach romping and play.

On Sunday evening, just before making the drive back to Toronto, Tina and Tickles made one last trip to their beach getaway and although Tina knew full well that winter's grip was probably just days away, as soon as the car door was opened, Tickles bounded onto the beach as if it was the middle of summer. With the leash in her hand Tina chased after the playful dog with a measure of fun in her call for Tickles to wait. When Tina stepped onto the beach, the fun turned suddenly sour as she found her dog seated in the sand, head hung low and hair raised on her spine. She was growling in a low tone and alternately whimpering. It was a tone that Tina had never seen out of Tickles–not even at the vet's office. For a moment she thought that the dog had stepped on something sharp or had somehow been injured, then Tina suddenly saw what Tickles was looking at. Standing just around a sharp bend in the beach and not more than a stone's throw from Tina and her dog was a man. His clothing was tattered and he appeared to be shoeless and up to his knees in the water. Tina's first thought was that this was an odd place to find a homeless person hanging around. Her second thought was to leave. Grabbing Tickles' collar, Tina snapped on the leash and began to pull, but the dog refused to move. Now nearly in a panic, Tina tugged at the dog and reached down as if to carry her. Tickles snarled loudly and put her ears back as if to strike a vicious bite. Tina lurched back and at that instant a deep cold voice spoke nearly into the back of her ear.

BEACHCOMBING FOR ETERNITY

"They've taken my money." The voice said.

Tina could feel the presence of the man within inches of her neck and instinctively she spun around. The man was simply gone and all that was there was the lake, the beach and a whimpering Tickles the dog. As Tina stood there, momentarily puzzled, the leash in her hand suddenly snapped tight, nearly pulling her over. Tickles was headed back to the car and no human holding onto a leather leash was going to slow her down. In a heartbeat, both Tickles and Tina were in a desperate run for the car. As fast as can be imagined the car was started, the doors were locked and they were speeding non-stop toward Toronto. Tickles cowered in the footwell of the passenger's seat all the way home and refused to look out the window.

Tickles and Tina were not the first beachcombers to come face to face with Louis Stonehouse. In fact, folks have been running into him, on occasion, since November of 1880. It was then that Louis took up residence on Weller's Beach for eternity.

To say that Louis Stonehouse was a penny pincher would probably be an understatement. He was a person to whom the value of keeping a dollar was far more important than the value of spending a dollar. It is said that he always wore a money belt and it contained every dollar that he had ever earned. When he was hired as the first mate aboard the schooner *Garibaldi* he brought his miserly ways and his money belt with him. Of course, the first mate was not paid as much as a captain, but in this era, captains were often the vessel's owner and so their money was always at risk should the vessel be wrecked or its cargo become damaged. The mate, on the other hand, would earn more than the deck crew and had none of his income at risk. Louis Stonehouse was sure that if the *Garibaldi* wrecked, he would be able to keep all of his money–he was wrong.

On a wicked mid-November day in 1880, both Louis Stonehouse and the *Garibaldi* were headed across the surface of Lake Ontario into the teeth of a fierce gale. Sharp waves pounded incessantly against the bow of the schooner and burst into ice cold showers of spray that began to freeze upon the deck. The temperature had dropped almost twenty degrees in the last dozen hours and it appeared as if winter was here with all of its angry rage. Spotting the flashes of the Presqu'ile Point lighthouse the *Garibaldi's* captain knew he was nearing Wellers Bay and decided to run for shelter there.

"This blow's only gonna get worser' so we may as well make a run behind the point." The captain shouted through the wind toward Louis.

The wind seemed to favor a run into the bay and the mate went about helping the crew make sails for the dash to safety. But it was a rude trick that Lake Ontario was about to play upon the *Garibaldi* and her crew. No sooner had the sail been set and the boat had been heeled into a fine sailing stance than the gale suddenly swung around and began to blow from off of the bow. Now with her teeth in the wind the *Garibaldi* would have to tack a zigzag course to reach safety and that would be just too much for the 17-year-old boat. Soon she was taking water into her hold and the crew could not manage the sails and pumps well enough to keep her afloat. In desperation, the captain ordered the sails down and the anchors dropped. The *Garibaldi* had ridden out many a storm like this and there was no reason to believe that today would be different. Once the hooks were over the side and the sails properly stowed, the crew could concentrate on the pumps until the storm blew itself out.

With a matter-of-fact confidence, the crew of the *Garibaldi* went to work at dropping her hooks and soon the huge anchors went over the side and grappled at the bottom of the lake. Next the crew turned their attention to the *Garibaldi's* pumps. No sooner had they started gaining on the water in her hold, then it became obvious that the hooks had not taken hold and the schooner was dragging anchor toward the sandbar. Through the raging surf the *Garibaldi's* crew could see the nearby wreck of the schooner *Belle Scheridan*. Just ten days earlier she had gone a wreck on the sandbar and only one of her crew had survived. When the keel of the *Garibaldi* went grinding onto the bar, every member of her crew had the wreck of the *Belle Scheridan* in mind. It did not take much convincing to get most of them mustered at the yawl boat ready to abandon ship. Nearly everyone, including the captain, was willing to depart the boat yet there was a single man who refused to leave, and that was Louis Stonehouse.

For reasons known only to him, Louis stood firmly at the wheel as the rest of the crew made haste toward the beach. The last time that Louis was seen alive he was ducking into the deckhouse as if to retire to his bunk. The remainder of the *Garibaldi's* crew landed safely on the beach and headed toward civilization. Meanwhile the gale intensified, the temperature dropped well below freezing and the *Garibaldi* was beaten into submission by Lake Ontario. The following day the lake was still running high as the *Garibaldi's* crew, accompanied by a group of local residents returned to the beach opposite the wreck. It was still far too rough to launch a boat and go out to the wreck and find poor Louis, yet everyone standing on the beach knew his fate. What they didn't know was why he had refused to come ashore.

Later that evening several members of the crew of the *Garibaldi* were warming seats in a local saloon and the topic of Louis's reasoning became the subject of conversation.

BEACHCOMBING FOR ETERNITY

"He probably didn't want to leave his precious money." One crewman sneered.

The subject of his money belt and the speculation of how much cash he may have stashed in his bunk was freely tossed about by the crewmen and nearby ears were keen to listen to the details. Just before dawn the following morning two ne'er-do-wells rowed across a cold, but calm Lake Ontario and out to the wreck of the *Garibaldi*. The boat was sunken with her decks awash and her hull twisted in agonizing death. Sails hung tattered and lines were askew as the two men made their way across her deck and toward the companionway door in her stern cabin. As they entered the darkened deckhouse the feeling was like that of a big wooden icebox and the sight that greeted them was like something from a nightmare. There, up to his hips in water, gazing directly at the doorway as if waiting for a rescuer to enter, stood Louis Stonehouse–frozen solid. It was a sight that would scare any decent person out of their wits, but no decent person would come aboard to rob the dead. In a hustle, grimy fingers peeled back the frozen clothing of the *Garibaldi's* first mate and in short order his precious money belt was removed and he was left alone once more.

Sometime later that same day a group of better meaning men rowed out and removed the mate's body. Louis was later escorted to his proper burial ashore and the shipwreck fell into history. Of course, the thoughts of cash are not as easily put aside as the thoughts of a shipwreck. In the days that followed there was a great deal of quiet talk about the fact that Louis may have concealed a large amount of cash somewhere in the cabin of the wrecked *Garibaldi*. On several occasions strange lights were seen hovering around the wreck at night and many folks thought that these were the lamps of looters searching the wreck. Others came to a more frightening conclusion. The lights, they said, were the lamps of the dead who were protecting the wreck and its hidden loot.

One fine Indian summer afternoon a couple of local fellows decided to "pay a visit to the wreck" and find out what was causing those strange lights. Jumping into a small rowboat they pulled out to the wreck and climbed aboard. The lake had taken its toll on the boat in the previous weeks and anything that could be broken, had been broken. The hull groaned and swayed freely with the slightest of waves as the boarding party made their way to the deckhouse. When they pushed open the companionway door, they came face to face with the ghost of Louis Stonehouse, standing exactly where he had died! Stumbling over one another it only took the men a few seconds to get away from the door and dash to their rowboat. As they attempted to set a speed record for rowing away from the wreck they heard a mournful voice cry "They've taken my money!"

When the two amateur investigators finally reached the beach they made tracks for town. Once there, they told their story, but no one was willing to believe them. Insistently they challenged others to duplicate their adventure. The results were the same. When the investigating wreck walkers entered the tattered cabin of the *Garibaldi* they came face to face with the ghost of the boat's former first mate. From then on, the local folks stayed away from the *Garibaldi's* wreck. Eventually a salvage team arrived and recovered the *Garibaldi* from the sandbar. After a good deal of patching and pumping, the wreck was hauled away and returned to service. Oddly, the wreckers said nothing of the ghost or his money. They simply recovered the boat and departed. The wreck of the *Belle Sheridan,* however was beyond repair and no effort was ever made to remove her bones. For many years thereafter, the strange light was seen hovering over her grave.

Many years after the wrecks of that November in 1880, the ghost stories had faded from the local memory. It was then that folks began reporting encounters with the ghost of Louis Stonehouse on the beach. His spirit walks the sands in search of his missing money which was spent over a century ago by others less frugal and less honest. Day or night, he appears unexpectedly every now and then–a tattered beachcomber–searching for a hoard that he will never find. Perhaps he is there, right now, walking the beach yet leaving no tracks.

ICE LIGHTS

To folks who live near the Great Lakes, ownership of a cottage or "place on the lake" is a symbol of success and status. So it follows that those who are successful in life buy property on the lake shore. If you happen to be a person who does not own a place on the lake, the invitation to come and stay at someone else's place is nearly impossible to turn down, even in the dead of winter.

Rose was a senior worker on an office staff at a Detroit area manufacturing company. As such, she had her choice of vacation periods and normally took two weeks in the summer to drive across the nation with her retired husband and attend an annual camping event. They had been participating in this annual outing for nearly 15 years without failure and it had become a huge part of their life. Then came the summer when a contract at the company that Rose worked for suffered some complications and it was quite likely that the entire company could go under if the job was not reworked and the contract issues resolved. Suddenly there was talk of cancelled vacations. There were only three people in line to get cancelled and one of them was Rose. She made it quite clear to her supervisor that she would quit before she would miss out on her annual outing simply because someone else had screwed up a contract.

One advantage to working for a small company is that when big problems happen the people involved can sometimes settle the issue personally with the owner. So it was that Rose found herself looking over her desk directly at the owner of the company who invited her to meet with him in his office. Before the door to the owner's office was fully closed, Rose started to flatly state her position, but the boss stopped her in mid protest. He informed her that he was well aware of her annual plans and that he knew full well that she was willing to quit before missing her trip. He also told her that she was a critical link in the process of saving the company in this troubled time. Then he offered her a compromise. It was a package that included a healthy year-end bonus, an extra week of vacation the following year, his personal guarantee that she would not miss next year's trip and to sweeten the deal a week's stay with her spouse at the boss' vacation home up on Lake Superior for Valentine's Day. Rose said she would think about it.

That afternoon as the office staff gathered in the break room, Rose detailed her meeting as the rest of the employees listened intently. She scoffed at going up on the Superior shore in February, but one of the other employees spoke up and asked if she had ever been up there during that time of year. Rose admitted that she had not, but that it must be unimaginably cold.

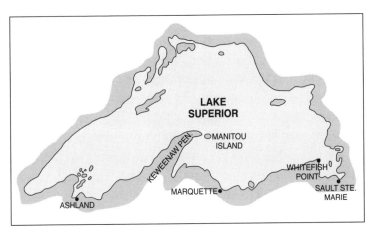

Her fellow employee stated that it was indeed cold, but it was also fantastically beautiful and wonderfully isolated. Then the others began to speculate as to just how nice the company owner's vacation house would be and suddenly Rose began to get a giddy feeling in her stomach. Perhaps this was a pretty sweet deal after all. Later she pitched the deal over the phone to her husband, Ken, who was more than willing to do it. By the end of the workday, Rose strolled into the boss' office and told him that he had a deal.

The contract was repaired and the company was saved and Rose was so busy that she hardly missed her annual outing at all. As the autumn turned into winter and the holidays came and went, Rose found that all of her holiday shopping had been well covered by her bonus–which was far beyond what she had expected. Soon the winter pushed into its darkest depths as the suburban streets of Detroit were garnished with piles of dirty snow and the cars were painted in salt. In the gloom of the afternoon before Rose's winter adventure to the Superior shore, the company owner stopped by her desk and dropped off the keys to the vacation house. He explained that his nephew had just come back from three weeks up there and that the place was ready for Rose and her husband. The refrigerator was stocked, the firewood was stacked and the satellite TV was working fine. She was ordered to have a relaxing time and to help herself to anything. He also told her that a number was on the kitchen board and if she needed anything at all to call the local caretaker who would be at her service. Then he added that the caretaker lived in a small town about 45 minutes from the vacation house. Of course, that was the nearest civilization too. The following morning Rose and her husband Ken had the car packed and soon were headed up I-75 toward the great white north.

The drive toward the vacation home took advantage of a clear crisp winter day. The interstate highway was clean and dry and when they departed the main road and headed up toward the Superior shore they were both astounded at the depth of the snow in Michigan's Upper Peninsula. The plowed roadway was often more like a tunnel and they wondered how anyone could live up here. The road leading to the vacation house was snowy but passable and Ken commented that if the weather set in, they may well be stuck up there until spring. Rose was having second thoughts of her own until they wheeled onto the property where the boss' vacation home was located. The sun was just beginning to set and the ice on the lake extended as far as the eye could see but reflected the orange of the setting sun. It was a stunning site and the house was a stunning structure. It was over three times larger than their own home and there seemed to be windows everywhere–most of which took advantage of the view of the lake. Indeed, Rose assured herself that she had made a good deal.

They spent that evening settling in and getting to know the place. Rose explored every inch of the house and inspected every amenity. Her husband pondered building a fire in the fireplace, but then distracted himself with the satellite TV. Long after Rose had decided to retire for the night her spouse was awake, busily clicking away at the remote control and watching stations of every description. By midnight he decided he too should turn in for the night. As he turned off the remaining lights and the TV, he noticed something outside the window. Squinting into the distance, he saw a series of amber colored lights far out on the lake. He said to himself that he never knew that the big lakeboats were running this time of the year and then went off to bed.

A pleasant atmosphere hung over the vacation home the following day. The winter sun was bright and every inch of the shore was coated in a frosty white. Out on the lake the cakes of ice had been shoved and piled upon themselves in huge wind rows and they seemed to hang on the shore like giant ice cliffs. The entire lake was a rugged ice-flow, like a huge pile of broken glass plates each being several feet thick. Later in the day Rose and her husband bundled up and ventured down to the ice. They stood there amazed as the ice made low groans and subtle cracking sounds as if it were a huge sleeping monster. That day both Rose and her spouse learned a new sense of just how big and powerful Lake Superior is.

Near dinner time there came an unexpected knock at the door. Rose answered and found herself face-to-face with a smiling local man who introduced himself as Geoff the caretaker. He had stopped by to see if everything was in order when the couple arrived and to find out if they had any questions. During the course of this conversation, Rose's spouse mentioned that he was surprised that the big lakeboats were still sailing at this time of the year and how he had always thought that they laid up in the winter. Geoff shook his head and stated flatly that there "ain't no boats this time of the year." Ken told him he had seen some lights last night and was sure there had been a boat out there. After some consideration Geoff said he would call his brother-in-law down at the Soo and find out. He said his brother-in-law worked at the locks and could tell him what boats were running. Rose told Geoff not to go to any trouble because her husband was likely seeing things. Her spouse retreated by saying that maybe he had seen some lights from an island or something. Geoff snickered that the only land in that direction was Caribou Island and it was 50 miles away.

After building a nice fire, Ken spent the evening still fascinated with the satellite TV. Rose, on the other hand, spent her time exploring every volume stored in the vacation home's library. Just before eight o'clock that evening the phone rang and on the other end of the line was Geoff the caretaker. He told Rose that he had just spoken to his brother-in-law and indeed there were no lakeboats out on Superior. In fact, they were not even expected to start sailing again for another month. Rose gleefully taunted her spouse with that information, and insisted that if he did not stop seeing things she was going to have him carted away to the nuthouse. He simply grunted in response and kept exercising his remote control finger. When Rose got back into the library she took a second to look out toward the darkness of the frozen lake. There in the distance was the string of lights that her husband had reported. She scurried back to the den and told him what she had seen and both of them pressed up against the window to witness the lights.

Rose was not one to be tempted by curiosity, because she was like an addicted gambler and could not stop investigating until she had her answer. She remembered seeing a large telescope in the upstairs sitting room and both her and her spouse made a hustle to get up there to it. It took some manipulation, but finally they managed to aim the telescope at the lights. The window glass of the house was apparently distorting the image as all that the lights appeared to be were amber blobs no matter how they focused the telescope. They decided to put on their jackets and move the telescope out onto the deck for a more clear view. Even with the aid of the telescope the lights were too far away to reveal anything more than their order, but that was enough. It appeared to be not one, but two boats, each with lower lights and taller lights as if suspended from masts. One boat's lamps were bright while the other's were far more dim. It was too cold to remain outside very long so the couple retreated to the warmth of the indoors. Through the evening, however, they kept a casual watch toward the lights on the ice. Then, just after midnight, as Ken was again turning off the TV and heading for bed he looked out and saw that the lights were gone.

In the daylight of the next day, Ken turned his attention away from the satellite TV and toward the telescope. The day was clear and the visibility should have been unlimited. For nearly two hours he scanned the distance of frozen Lake Superior, but saw nothing but ice. That evening, near 10 o'clock the lights suddenly reappeared and again after midnight they vanished. The following day a series of snow squalls obscured the lake as near white out conditions prevailed. Into the evening the snow kept coming and there was no chance that the lights could be seen. Ken crawled into bed and pondered the lights. Then he came up with an answer–it must be ice fishermen! Laying in bed he felt quite satisfied in his having apparently solved the mystery. Then he noticed a strange sound–a low howl in the distance. For a long time he listened as the howl pulsated. Finding his slippers he made his way to the sitting room and listened carefully. The distant sound was coming from outside. He opened the door and could clearly hear what sounded like the sobs of a steam whistle hooting frantically in the snowy distance. Then just as suddenly the sounds stopped. Ken wondered if there was more to this puzzle than he had calculated.

Ken and Rose could hardly wait for the light of the next day to expire. They were like two kids plotting to stay up late and not to take their eyes off of those lights. They played at "shooing" away every snow squall in the hope that the night would give them a continual view of the mystery lights. Rose prepared hot chocolate and they bundled up for protracted duty watching the lights from the deck. Lake Superior, however, was going to test them as it sent arctic cold winds screaming across its frozen surface. They were forced to abandon the telescope and simply watch from behind the windows while remaining warm in the sitting room. As if on cue, the lights appeared just before nine o'clock. Ken said that they looked as if they had risen from beneath the surface and both he and Rose took turns watching the lights almost without blinking. Just after midnight Rose saw the dim set of lights suddenly go out and half of the brighter lights also go out. She shouted to Ken who bounded to the window and both of them swore that they saw the remaining lights move. Then, suddenly, all of the lights were gone! Another element to their mystery had been added.

The following day Ken placed a call to Geoff and trying not to sound like a nut he explained what had been happening out on the lake. Geoff was interested and accepted an invitation to come and witness the lights himself that evening. He explained that no one without a death wish would be out on that ice fishing and he was more than curious to see the lights. That evening Geoff showed up, but so did old man winter. The night was still, but snow fell in the form of huge flakes and obscured any viewing of the lake. By half past 11 o'clock everyone agreed that it was a lost cause and after exchanging pleasantries, Geoff headed out the door. Rose and Ken were lamenting their missed opportunity when there came a pounding at the door. It was Geoff who was excitedly, inviting them to come out and "listen!" As they all stood in the drive, they could hear that old steam whistle frantically hooting again in the distance as clear as can be. Excitedly they all huffed around to the lake side of the house and then stood still and listened. The hooting continued as they gleefully asked one another what it was. Then suddenly it was gone, as if swallowed up by the snowy night. All three of the witnesses shook their heads in disbelief.

Lake Superior concealed the mystery lights for the rest of Rose and Ken's stay. The next night was windswept and filled with pelting snow and on the morning of their departure Rose and Ken were sorry to leave without having solved the puzzle. All the way home they speculated as to what the lights were and what was making that whistle hoot. When Rose went to return the keys to the vacation home, the boss asked how her stay had been, she could not hold back and gushed with every detail of their encounter with the strange lights and hooting whistle. Then she suddenly realized that her boss probably thought she was suffering from cabin fever! She shut up and tried to dismiss her own story. The boss simply grinned in a wide smile and said "That's living on the shipwreck coast. Sounds like you were lucky enough to meet one of Superior's ghost ships." It was sort of what Rose and Ken had already decided. To this day, however, they don't know for sure.

NO TRESPASSING

Although many of the stories in this text are long and spooky, this one is short and sweet. The reasoning for that is because it is a story of some illegal trespassing and general stupidity that led to a ghostly encounter. Many people have stories of ventures up on the abandoned ore docks that mark the harbors of the Lake Superior shore, but the person who passed along this story has asked that his name be changed so as to prevent his being marked as an idiot. For that reason we will simply refer to him as "Tim" and thus only those who were along with him on that drunken night will know his true identity.

It was the mid 1990s and the midst of a fine summer holiday weekend. For Tim and his pals there had been far too much fun and a bit too much drinking to remain sensible. In the town of Superior, Wisconsin such fine summer holidays are normally spent boating, either on Allouez and Superior bays, or out on Lake Superior itself. Such boating should always be done in a sober condition, unless you are admittedly stupid like Tim and his friends. As darkness fell upon their day of water

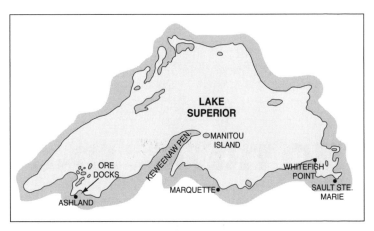

skiing and beer drinking the bunch decided to go have a late night campfire on one of the old abandoned ore docks. After obtaining more beer, the band set out for the huge structure by way of their speedboat. It was the best way to avoid those pesky fences and "No Trespassing" signs that block access from shore.

The gigantic abandoned Great Northern ore docks and the Northern Pacific ore dock are a part of the Superior Wisconsin landscape. Established in the late 1800s, the docks evolved and grew to serve the fleet of Great Lakes oreboats that fed the industry of the 20th century. Today, each dock stretches a half mile long and stands 80-feet tall. These docks were designed to feed natural ore by gravity into the holds of the big lakeboats. Iron ore is amazingly dense and so a single train load of it is very difficult to move up high enough to then be gravity fed into a vessel. For that reason, wooden trestles lead from the docks and form an inclined plain that reaches several miles through the city of Superior. Atop each dock there is enough room to allow four trains to stand upon it side by side.

The ore was dropped through the bottoms of the hopper cars and allowed to fall into the storage pockets of the dock. Laborers were employed to use long steel poles and shovels and while standing on top of the rail cars shove the ore as it was being emptied from the cars and cause it to flow more freely. These laborers were normally Scandinavian immigrants and more than a few of them met their death by falling either from the railcar to the ground or into the ore pocket itself. Each ore pocket on each dock could hold a total of 327 tons of iron ore. The ore would slide down chutes that were lowered into a boat's hold, each pocket having its own chute. When the docks were active, a lakeboat would simply tie up beneath the chutes and the ore would flow in as fast as gravity could pull it.

Over the years the assorted ore ports around Lake Superior all found the need to construct ore docks. Places such as Marquette, Ashland and Duluth all serviced the lakeboats with these giant docks. Made of

Long abandoned, the ore docks at Superior are an inviting place for the curious and the reckless. Author's Collection

tons of reinforced concrete and acres of treated timber the structures were built to withstand anything that mother nature could throw at them. Indeed they have survived autumn storms and winter ice for more than a century. Yet the one thing that they could not survive was economic evolution and advancing technology.

Abandonment of the docks resides in the fact that "natural" iron ore, which looks very much like red rock, has a high degree of moisture in it. This moisture content would often cause problems in loading during the late shipping season. Temperatures in the Lake Superior region would often drop below freezing in the early autumn and the result would eventually be that the ore would freeze in the pockets while waiting to be loaded. The cure for this was to run steam hoses into the pockets and attempt to thaw the ore. It was a process that took a great deal of time and was very dangerous. The problem was solved with the advent of taconite pellets. These pellets consist of low grade iron ore that is ground into a fine powder and then formed into marble sized pellets which are then fired like pottery. This material is far easier to handle and ship than natural ore. There is practically no residual moisture in taconite and so it does not freeze in the pockets and can easily be shipped year round if needed. Also, there was no longer a need to employ dozens of laborers to shove the ore. Taconite simply flowed like marbles and was easily dumped from the hopper cars. The result was that hundreds of ore-shovers found themselves out of work. Eventually the docks themselves would soon follow the ore-shovers into obscurity.

In the city of Superior the advent of taconite and the construction of a new taconite loading dock to the south of the old ore docks combined with the decline in the American steel industry spelled the end for the giant ore docks. As the 1980s began, the steel industry was beginning to exclusively use taconite as its ore of choice. Additionally, the new super-lakers were showing up in greater numbers. This class of vessel was dominated by the 1000-footers and with their beams of 105-feet they would not fit into the slips of the old docks. Additionally, it would take over 172 of the old ore dock's pockets to fill a single 1000-foot lakeboat. The old docks at Superior were suddenly outdated and were subsequently abandoned.

For years the docks of Superior stood silent. To this day, no one can figure out what to do with them. If the city were to demolish the structures they will be left with huge piles of wreckage that would cost millions of dollars to clear and haul away. The docks themselves can serve no other function other than that for which they were constructed. Thus, the most economical

Seen from inside, the Superior ore dock seems to stretch into the distance like a cathedral to the industrial revolution. Author's Collection

solution to the problem is to simply leave them standing. Of course, that is an open invitation to stupid people.

Tim and his pals pulled their boat up to the end of the Northern Pacific dock and climbed onto the base. Standing on the outer edge of the lower pier Northern Pacific dock, the first thing Tim noticed was how narrow the cement wharf that runs around the dock seemed to be. In his drunken state the cement pier seemed to roll like a ship at sea. The pillars upon which the dock stands run along each side of the structure and tower overhead. These pillars are three feet wide and 12-feet thick and are made of stacked concrete forms that are each about one foot tall. The open legs of these pillars are over 40-feet tall and all of the pillars are spaced on 12-foot centers. Stepping into the dock's center, Tim found his world was a strange silent place. The footing of each dock pillar is an elongated half pyramid of formed concrete that extends down more than six feet. Overall the Northern Pacific dock contains more than 350 of these huge pillars. Uniquely, the Northern Pacific dock is divided into two sections. The first third of the dock, which is the section that is the closest to the land, is the "old" original section of the dock and the last two thirds of the structure is the later section of the dock. The difference being the ore pockets of the old section are huge iron cylinders that are 12-feet in diameter and 25-feet tall. That is about the size of a steam locomotive tipped up on end. There are 51 of these huge pockets on each side of the Northern Pacific dock's old section. The new section is a solid wall of formed concrete that stands just over 30-feet tall. At its base and directly adjacent to each pillar is the opening through which the ore poured into the chutes. Although some of the chutes still remain on the old Burlington Northern docks, all of the chutes have been removed from the Northern Pacific dock. Between the pillars the inside of the dock is roofed by the cement underside of the ore pockets. These pockets are angled to allow the ore within to slide, so when Tim looked up at the underside of the dock the appearance was that of a huge cement cathedral with a 70-foot high peak. This cathedral-like tunnel runs for a distance of nearly a half mile. The floor of the dock is a carpet of spilled iron ore and Tim and his pals dumped their party goods on a nice dry spot near the end of the dock. Had they bothered to look at the ground in a sober condition they would have found that in a single sweep of the hand, several different grades of ore can be scooped up. Exploring a bit, Tim found an area where the weather had washed out some of the spilled ore. It was a good indication of just how much iron ore was shipped from this dock over the last century. There it could be seen that the carpet of spilled ore is over three feet thick! This means that so much iron ore was shipped from this dock that the spillage alone makes up a layer on the dock that is three feet thick and a half mile long. No doubt that a geology buff could take a core sample here, and from it, watch as the grades of iron ore that were mined in this region had changed over the last century. Tim's concern, of course, was beer and a campfire. Gathering anything that was made of wood, the drunken campers made a small fire and proceeded to squat around it.

Soon the talk in the party turned to climbing the dock and seeing what is on top. The night was clear and warm and before long "dares" and "double dares" were being tossed around. No one in their right mind would try to climb one of these docks, but now being beer can stupid, Tim was clearly not in his right mind. He took up the dares and decided to climb the dock. The original stairway that allowed access to the top of the dock consisted of a zigzag iron framework with wooden steps that were supported by long angle-iron holds. Those wooden steps were removed before the dock had been abandoned and now there was only the angle-iron on which to step. A century of rust and weathering should have scared Tim off before he reached the first level, but it did not. Giggling nervously he made his way hand over hand and higher and higher until the top was closer than the ground. An ounce too much pull on any single bolt or iron fitting would have sent Tim to a drunken grave, but he had left his common sense in a discarded beer can earlier in the day. Scraping knees and cutting fingers–all the way to the top he went. Finally he shimmied atop the great ore dock, completely satisfied in his stupidity and never thinking about the simple fact that now he would have to get back down again.

Standing more than 80-feet off the ground Tim belted out a drunken "yahoo" from the top of the Northern Pacific ore dock and out into the moonlit night. Far below, his friends shouted up a "So long Tim!" as they could be seen piling into the speed boat, intent on leaving poor Tim behind in a drunken joke. He could care less, he was on top of the world and figured to look around a bit and see what was up there. It would be a short tour.

No sooner did Tim turn his attention away from his departing pals and around toward the length of the dock than he found himself face-to-face with someone else! Standing a dozen feet away and looking like a cross between a hermit and an angry night watchman, was the figure of a man. At first Tim thought that he had been caught trespassing and would have some embarrassed explaining to do, but an instant later he saw that he was facing something much worse. The man's face was ashen white and a long bushy mustache was growing beneath his bulbous nose. His deep-set eyes seemed to glow a strange orange with an anger the likes of which Tim had never before witnessed. He was wearing a floppy peaked hat and a tattered coat and most impressively, he was gripping a large shovel in his scraggly hands. Tim began to babble an explanation of why he had climbed the dock when the man suddenly lunged toward him. Growling the man shouted at Tim in some sort of foreign language as the drunken trespasser instinctively stepped back. Then with a swift swipe the man swung the shovel as if to plant the blade on the side of Tim's head! Tim ducked and swore as the shovel passed by just missing him with a "whoosh" sound. Stumbling backward he fell and found himself scooting toward the edge of the dock as the man raised the shovel high into the night and prepared to brain the drunken trespasser. Tim raised his arm across his face and waited for the impact. A long moment passed and then Tim slowly lowered his arm and peeked over his elbow. The man was gone.

Instantly Tim decided that on top of the Northern Pacific ore dock was not the place where he wanted to be. In the darkness he fumbled back to the dilapidated stairway that had brought him to this level of stupidity and began a hasty climb back down. In a near panic he made his way down. For a moment he thought that perhaps the man at the top had fallen and was laying dead down below. Or maybe he had slipped and dropped into one of the ore storage pockets. It mattered little to Tim, he simply wanted to be off of that dock as fast as possible. When his foot hit the ground he scurried around a bit like a panicked mouse then ran to the edge of the wharf and screamed toward his departing pals who were laughing about in the boat, which was drifting about 50-feet out in the bay. He screamed for them to come back but they teased him in reply. So with that he took a running start and dove headlong into the water and proceeded to set a world record for drunken swimming. When his friends pulled him from the water they thought for a moment that the shivering and screaming Tim had been injured. He kept thrashing around and saying things about the guy with the shovel. Pressing the boat's motor to full throttle they headed into the night and places where there are clearer details.

Once the crew of drunks were ashore and the boat safely trailered, the now relatively sobered Tim sat in the bed of a pal's pickup truck in near shock. Shaking uncontrollably he told the story over and over again. There was some discussion about what to do. After all, if there was an old man on the dock who fell, the police should be called and the incident properly reported. Of course, then how would they explain that while they were drunk, boating and trespassing they had driven this old crazy man to his death? All agreed that they would be better off to just keep quiet and see if anything came out in the papers or the news. As the summer faded away, there was never any story of any missing person or any body being found. Tim kept thinking that if the guy had fallen into one of those storage pockets he could lay there forever and not be discovered. Then again, the guy was about to clobber him, so maybe it served him right. He briefly gave thought to climbing back up in the daylight and taking another look around, but was sure that he would never be drunk enough to do such a thing again. A few years later Tim was at work and swapping stories with the rest of the guys on his crew when the story of the man with the shovel came up. One of the fellows working with Tim shrugged and said, "Sounds like ya' saw a ghost." Tim suddenly realized that he may have indeed seen a ghost.

Over the years I have talked to a number of people who were dumb enough to try and climb one of those old ore docks. Often their stories involve too many adult beverages and too little sense. Most have only gotten a short distance up the walkways before fear sends them back down. It is important to remember that fear is a good instinct and that attempting to climb these structures can end your life. Perhaps Tim encountered nothing more than his own fear that night. Then again, maybe he came upon someone who learned the hard way that these old ore docks are deadly places and no trespassing is allowed.

GLOSSARY

Abeam: Directly beside a vessel

Aft: Toward the rear of a vessel

Back: A ship's spine or keel

Barge: A vessel that has no power of its own and must be towed

Beam: The width of a vessel

Beam ends: The sides of a vessel

Boat: On the Great Lakes, a ship is called a boat

Bulkhead: A wall-like partition that divides a boat's hull

Bunker: A compartment where a boat's fuel is stored

Capstan: Device used for pulling lines or chains

Dock Whollopers: Laborers

Firehold: The part of the engine room where the boiler fires are fed

Fo'c'sle: The raised part of a boat's bow containing crew quarters

Founder: To sink in a disastrous way

Funnel: A steamer's smokestack

Hawser: A tow line, steel or rope

Heel: To lean to one side

Keel: A supporting beam that runs the length of a boat's bottom

Lay-up: Out of service for season or repairs

List: A tilt to one side

Lighter: To raise a sunken boat by removing its cargo

Lumber hooker: A small vessel used for hauling lumber, its name is said to have come from the fact that assorted hooks and lines were often used to load and unload the cargo

Oreboat: Boats designed to carry ore of any type

Ore dock: Where ore boats tie up to take on ore

Port side: Left side

Saltie: An ocean going vessel that visits the lakes

Schooner-barge: A sailing vessel that is usually towed

Screw: Propeller

Spardeck: The maindeck through which cargo is loaded

Stern: Back of vessel

Texas deck: The deck atop which the pilothouse is mounted

Windlass: Used to raise anchor

Yawl: A small rowboat or lifeboat

ABOUT THE AUTHOR

Author W. Wes Oleszewski was born and raised in mid-Michigan and spent most of his life with an eye turned toward the Great Lakes. In the past 12 years he has authored 11 books on the subject of Great Lakes maritime history and lighthouses.

W. Wes Oleszewski
Great Lakes Maritime Author
and Research Historian

Noted for his meticulous research, Oleszewski has a knack for weeding out the greatest of details from the most obscure events and then weaving those facts into the historical narratives which are his stories. His tales of actual events are real enough to thrill any reader while every story is technically correct and highly educational. Oleszewski feels that the only way to teach history in this age of computer and video games is through "narrative." Along the researcher's path, this author has also become acquainted, sometimes first-hand, with the multitude of ghosts and ghost stories that haunt the history of the lakes. The final product of his efforts are captivating books that can be comfortably read and enjoyed by everyone from the eldest grandmother to the grade-school kid and future historian.

Born on the east side of Saginaw, Michigan in 1957, Wes Oleszewski attended public school in that city through grade nine, when his family moved to the town of Freeland, Michigan. In 1976 he graduated from Freeland High School and a year later entered the Embry-Riddle Aeronautical University in Daytona Beach, Florida. Working his way through college by way of his own earned income alone, Oleszewski graduated in 1988 with a commercial pilot's certificate, "multi-engine and instrument airplane" ratings as well as a B.S. Degree in Aeronautical Science. Along with his writing, he has pursued a career as a professional pilot. He holds an A.T.P. certificate and to date has logged more than 5,000 hours of flight time most of which is in airline category and jet aircraft. Samples of his writing can be found on his website at www.lighthouses-lakeboats.com.

Other Wes Oleszewski titles by Avery Color Studios, Inc.

- *True Tales of Ghosts & Gales,*
  Mysterious Great Lakes Shipwrecks
- *Stormy Disasters,*
  Great Lakes Shipwrecks
- *Ice Water Museum*
  Forgotten Great Lakes Shipwrecks
- *Ghost Ships, Gales & Forgotten Tales*
  True Adventures On The Great Lakes
- *Mysteries and Histories,*
  Shipwrecks of the Great Lakes
- *Great Lakes Lighthouses,*
  American & Canadian
- *Lighthouse Adventures*
  Heroes, Haunts & Havoc
  On The Great Lakes

Avery Color Studios, Inc. has a full line of Great Lak
oriented books, puzzles, cookbooks, shipwreck ai
lighthouse maps, lighthouse posters and Fresnel lens mod

For a free full-color catalog, call **1-800-722-9925**

Avery Color Studios, Inc. products are
available at gift shops and bookstores
throughout the Great Lakes region.